Round the World in Eighty Days

JULES VERNE

Level 5

Translated and retold by H. E. Palmer
Series Editors: Andy Hopkins and Jocelyn Potter

Pearson Education Limited
Edinburgh Gate, Harlow,
Essex CM20 2JE, England
and Associated Companies throughout the world.

ISBN: 978-1-4058-6518-0

First published in the Longman Simplified English Series 1937
First published in the Longman Fiction Series 1993
This adaptation first published by Addison Wesley Longman 1996
First published by Penguin Books 1999
This edition published 2008

14

Text copyright © Penguin Books Ltd 1999
This edition copyright © Pearson Education Ltd 2008

Typeset by Graphicraft Ltd, Hong Kong
Set in 11/14pt Bembo
Printed in China
SWTC/14

Published by Pearson Education Ltd

Every effort has been made to trace the copyright holders and we apologise in advance for any
unintentional omissions. We would be pleased to insert the appropriate acknowledgement in any
subsequent edition of this publication.

For a complete list of the titles available in the Pearson English Readers series, please
visit www.pearsonenglishreaders.com. Alternatively, write to your local Pearson Education
office or to Pearson English Readers Marketing Department, Pearson Education,
Edinburgh Gate, Harlow, Essex CM20 2JE, England.

Contents

Contents

Introduction

Then they began to talk about how long it would take to go round the world. Most of them thought that three months would be needed, but Phileas Fogg said that eighty days would be enough.

Mr Stuart said that it was impossible, but Phileas Fogg said that he was ready to go round the world himself in eighty days; and that he was ready to start that same evening.

It is 1872 and Phileas Fogg, a quiet, orderly English gentleman, is living in London. His life is divided between his home and his club, and follows a daily pattern that never changes. His new servant, Passepartout, who has joined his service that same day, is looking forward to a quiet, settled existence. Then his master arrives home and announces that, as a result of a bet that he has made, they are leaving immediately for a high-speed trip round the world. A crazy race across continents and oceans follows as Phileas attempts to travel round the world in eighty days in order to win his bet. Not surprisingly, he meets with many dangers and unexpected delays. And there is a detective, Mr Fix, who wants to arrest him for a bank robbery in London. Will Phileas succeed in winning his bet? As time passes, it begins to seem less and less likely . . .

Jules Verne is often considered to be the father of science fiction. His most popular works, originally written in French, have been translated into many languages and read and enjoyed all around the world.

Verne was born in 1828 in Nantes, a port on the French Atlantic coast. He went to school there, but at the age of eleven he tried to run away to sea. When he had been brought home by his worried parents, he promised them that in future he would travel only in his imagination – and he did, in fact, write more than fifty very imaginative travel stories.

Verne's father was a judge, and always intended his son to follow in his footsteps. He therefore encouraged Jules to go to Paris to study law. However, by the time that he had completed his degree, Jules was sure that his interest and his future were not in the legal world at all, but in the world of literature. He began writing the words for songs in musical plays. More importantly, he wrote travellers' stories for a magazine called the *Musée des Familles*, which showed him the true direction of his talent. When his father discovered that Jules was writing instead of studying law, he immediately stopped all financial support for his son. Jules was forced to work in the financial world, which he hated (although he was quite good at it). During this period, he met the authors Victor Hugo and Alexandre Dumas, who offered him some advice on his writing. One of Verne's first plays was produced with the support of Alexandre Dumas, but it had little success.

In 1857 Verne married Honorine Morel, who had recently lost her husband. Honorine already had two young daughters, and Verne and Honorine then had a son of their own. Although Verne was earning only a very small amount from his writing, Honorine encouraged him to continue until he achieved success. Verne was an enthusiastic sailor until 1886, when he was shot in the leg by a young relative who was mentally ill; for the rest of his life he walked with difficulty. His last years were spent in Amiens, where he continued to write, and where he also played an active part in local government. In 1892, he was honoured by the French government for his lifetime of writing. Although he was seriously ill and half blind towards the end of his life, he worked until his death in March 1905. His funeral was attended by more than 5,000 people.

In 1862 life was a struggle for the thirty-year-old Verne. He was married, with a child, and he had not yet found anyone willing to accept his books. He had always been interested in new travel possibilities and had previously written about the opportunities for exploring Africa in a hot air balloon, so he wrote a novel called *Five Weeks in a Balloon*, but nobody was interested. It was returned to him several times with the same complaint: 'It's too scientific.' Fortunately, Verne had met and become friends with Pierre-Jules Hetzel, one of the most important people in the world of books in France at the time. (Hetzel was responsible for bringing out the books of many famous writers, including Victor Hugo and George Sand.) With Hetzel's help, Verne rewrote the story, making it less serious and more humorous. *Five Weeks in a Balloon* came out at last in 1863, and was a great success.

Verne had finally shown that he had found a popular way of writing about the subjects that interested him. In the following years he wrote many other adventure stories, the most famous of which are *A Journey to the Centre of the Earth* (1864), *Twenty Thousand Leagues Under the Sea* (1870) and *Round the World in Eighty Days* (1873). As a result of these three books in particular (which are known together as 'The Extraordinary Journeys'), Verne made enough money to spend the rest of life writing. Most of his wealth, however, came from the stage plays of *Round the World in Eighty Days* and a later book, *Michael Strogoff* (1876), which he wrote with Adolph d'Ennery.

During the 19th century, transport systems all around the world were developing very quickly. Steam was becoming important as a method of powering trains and ships, and this led to great changes in the way that people travelled. By the 1860s, thousands of kilometres of railway had been built across Europe and America, and main lines were planned in Asia and Africa. Travellers were excited by the possibilities that these new types of transport were offering them. Verne shared this excitement and communicated it successfully to his readers.

Round the World in Eighty Days is Verne's best-loved book. It has the winning combination of adventure in mysterious, far-away places, scientific discovery and humour. The story originally appeared in parts in the Paris newspaper *Le Temps*. As the story developed, it caused so much excitement among readers that many people believed that the bet and the journey described in the story were real. Ever since *Round the World in Eighty Days* appeared, people have been so enthusiastic about the story that they have frequently attempted to copy Phileas Fogg's journey in real life.

At the time of the story, many of the countries and places visited by Fogg and his companions – Suez, India, Singapore and Hong Kong – were controlled by Britain. This adds to the excitement of the story as Fogg is chased by British justice in the shape of Mr Fix, a detective who believes that Phileas is an escaping bank robber. Mr Fix is legally able to arrest Fogg in any of these places – if he can get an arrest warrant from London in time! The main interest in the story, however, is the excitement of the race against time which Phileas Fogg has set himself – a race which still fires the imagination of readers of all ages.

The story has been filmed several times; the earliest film was in 1914. Perhaps the most famous was made in Hollywood in 1956, with several world-famous singers and actors of the time happy to play very small parts. For example, the great singer Frank Sinatra is on screen for just a couple of minutes as a piano player. David Niven plays the part of Phileas Fogg. The most recent film of the story for cinema was in 2002, with Steve Coogan as the hero.

One reason for Jules Verne's continuing popularity today, more than a hundred years after his death, is his great ability to look into the future and see what possibilities science might bring. For example, in *Twenty Thousand Leagues Under the Sea*, Captain Nemo's underwater ship is powered by a chemical process that can get electricity from sea water. One character in the story says, 'Yes, my friends, I believe that water will one day be employed as fuel. Water will be the coal of the future.' When we look back now at what he wrote, we can see that many of his dreams of the future have become reality. He wrote of flying machines that could travel to the stars, aeroplanes that flew by using spinning blades, and ships that could move under water.

In 1863, the year of his first great success as a writer, Verne wrote a novel called *Paris in the 20th Century*. It is about a young man who lives in a world of tall, glass buildings, high-speed trains, gas-powered cars, calculators and a worldwide communication system. In spite of all these wonderful new inventions, the young man is unable to find happiness and meets a tragic end. Hetzel thought that the pessimistic nature of the story would damage Verne's career. He advised his friend not to bring the book out for another twenty years. Verne put the story in a safe place, and then forgot about it. It was discovered by his great-grandson in 1989, and went on sale in book shops for the first time in 1994.

Chapter 1   Mr Phileas Fogg and Passepartout

In the year 1872 Mr Phileas Fogg lived at Number 7 Savile Row, London. Mr Fogg was a member of the Reform Club,* but as he never spoke about himself, nobody knew much else about him. He was certainly English, a fine-looking English gentleman. He was never seen at the bank or any other financial institution in the city. He was unknown to the world of shipowners and shipping. He was not a businessman. He was not a farmer. He was not a scientist. He was not a writer. He seemed to have no business or trade.

Mr Fogg was a member of the Reform Club, and that was all.

As he seemed to be without friends, it may be wondered how he had come to be a member of the Reform Club. It was quite simple. The head of the bank at which he kept his accounts had put his name on the list of those who wished to become members, and he was accepted.

Was Phileas Fogg rich? Yes, certainly. But how he had made his fortune nobody knew, and Mr Fogg was not the sort of man to tell anybody. He did not spend much money, although he did not seem to be one of those people who were particularly interested in saving it.

He talked very little; in fact nobody could have talked less. There was no secret about his habits and his daily life, but as he always did exactly the same things in exactly the same way every day, people wondered more and more about him and his past life.

Had he travelled? Probably, since nobody seemed as familiar with the world as he did. He appeared to have the most exact

* Reform Club: one of a number of London clubs in which gentlemen who were voted in as members could spend time for a yearly charge.

knowledge of every country and town in the world. Sometimes when the members of the club talked about travellers who had disappeared or become lost in some distant or unknown place, Mr Fogg, in a few clear words, would explain what had probably happened to them. His explanations often proved to be quite correct. He was a man who must have travelled everywhere – at least in his mind and imagination.

What was quite certain was that for many years Phileas Fogg had not left London. Those who knew him a little better than others said that nobody had ever seen him anywhere except in London. Even in London the only place where he was seen out of doors was between his house and club. His only activities were reading the newspapers and playing cards. It was clear that Mr Fogg played not for money, but for the love of the game. For him a game of cards was a struggle, but a pleasant one.

Phileas Fogg, it appeared, had neither a wife nor children – which may happen to the most honest people. Nobody had ever heard of his father or mother, or whether he had brothers and sisters. He lived alone in his house in Savile Row, which nobody ever visited. Nothing was known about the inside of his house. One servant was enough to do the work. He had his meals at the club at exactly the same times every day, when he sat in the same room, at the same table, always alone. He only went home to sleep, always exactly at midnight.

His home in Savile Row was a simple one, but very comfortable. Since his habits were so regular, and he spent all day at his club, his servant's duties were light. But Phileas Fogg expected from his servant a very high degree of exactness and regularity.

◆

It was October 2nd. Mr Fogg had just dismissed his servant, John Foster. John Foster had been guilty of a very serious irregularity:

the hot water that he had brought to his master's room was only eighty-four degrees instead of eighty-six – an inexcusable mistake. The servant had to go. Mr Fogg was now waiting for his new servant, who was expected between eleven o'clock and half past eleven.

Phileas Fogg was sitting in his armchair, his two feet together, his hands on his knees, his body straight and his head high. He was looking at the clock – a beautiful clock showing the seconds, the minutes, the hours, the days and the years. When half past eleven struck, Mr Fogg, according to his usual habit, would leave the house and go to his club.

At that moment there was a knock at the door. John Foster appeared.

'The new servant,' he announced.

A young man of about thirty years of age came in and greeted Fogg respectfully.

'You are a Frenchman and your name is John?' asked Mr Fogg.

'*Jean*, if you don't mind,' answered the young man. 'Jean Passepartout.★ My name suits me very well because I can do all sorts of things. I believe I am a good and honest person but I have had many trades in my time. I have sung in the streets, I have been an acrobat and a dancer on a tightrope, and I have taught these subjects. In Paris I was an officer in the fire service, so I can tell you stories of some of the most famous fires in that city. I left France five years ago. Wishing to know something of life in English homes, I came to England as a servant. Finding myself now without a situation, I have come to you. I have heard that you, sir, lead the quietest and most regular life of any man in England. This will suit me very well for I, too, wish to lead a quiet life in the future, and even to forget my name of Passepartout.'

★ Passepartout: a French word meaning 'go anywhere' or 'fit anything'. It is used to describe a key that will fit any lock.

'You will suit me,' answered Mr Fogg. 'I have been told that you are a good servant and a man to be trusted. You know my conditions?'

'Yes, sir.'

'Very well. What is the time by your watch?'

'Twenty-five minutes past eleven,' answered Passepartout, pulling out of his pocket a very large silver watch.

'You are slow,' said Mr Fogg.

'Excuse me, sir, but that is impossible.'

'You are four minutes slow,' said Mr Fogg. 'But it does not matter so long as you know it. And now, from this moment – 11.29 in the morning, Wednesday, 2nd October, 1872 – you are in my service.'

Phileas Fogg took his hat with his left hand, put it on his head with a machine-like movement, and left the house without another word.

After he had put his right foot in front of his left 575 times, and his left foot 576 times in front of his right, he reached the fine building of the Reform Club. In the dining room there he took his usual place at his usual table. At 12.47 he got up and went into the reading room, where one of the servants gave him a copy of *The Times* newspaper. He read this until 3.45, when he took up the *Standard*, and read that until dinner. At 5.40 he was back again in the reading room, and gave his attention to the *Morning Chronicle*. Half an hour later he was joined by a few of the other members. They began talking about a great bank robbery that had taken place the day before, in which the robber had stolen fifty-five thousand pounds in bank notes.

'The bank will lose its money, I think,' said one of them, a man named Andrew Stuart.

'I don't think so,' said another, Thomas Flanagan. 'The thief will be caught before long. As all the ports are being carefully watched by the police, he will find it difficult to leave the country.'

'The *Morning Chronicle* thinks that the person who has taken the money is not an ordinary thief, but an educated man,' said Mr Fogg.

They went on talking about the chances of the robber being caught, and of the different ways in which he could escape from the country.

Some of the gentlemen said that the world was so large that, if he managed to leave the country, a robber could easily hide from those who were trying to catch him. But Phileas Fogg did not agree with them.

'The world,' he said, 'is no longer a big place. Fast ships and trains have changed everything. For example, we now have the Suez Canal, and there are railways running across India and the United States.'

Then they began to talk about how long it would take to go round the world. Most of them thought that three months would be needed, but Phileas Fogg said that eighty days would be enough.

To prove his claim, Mr Fogg took a piece of paper and wrote down:

London to Suez by Calais and Brindisi (railway and steamer)	7 days
Suez to Bombay (steamer)	13 "
Bombay to Calcutta (railway)	3 "
Calcutta to Hong Kong (steamer)	13 "
Hong Kong to Yokohama (steamer)	6 "
Yokohama to San Francisco (steamer)	22 "
San Francisco to New York (railway)	7 "
New York to London (steamer and railway)	9 "
	80 days

Mr Stuart said that it was impossible, and offered to bet four thousand pounds that he was right. Phileas Fogg said that he was ready to go round the world himself in eighty days; and that he was ready to start that same evening. He said that he would not only agree to the bet of four thousand pounds with Mr Stuart, but that he would be prepared to bet twenty thousand pounds of his fortune that he could go round the world in eighty days.

His five friends accepted the bet, and Mr Fogg warned them that they would have to pay for his journey.

'So that is agreed and arranged,' said Mr Fogg. 'I believe that a train leaves for Dover at 8.45 this evening. I shall travel by it.'

'This evening?' cried Mr Stuart, in a very surprised voice.

'This evening,' answered Fogg, as calmly as if it were a matter of going to the next street. 'As this is Wednesday, 2nd October, I ought to be back in the reading room of the Reform Club on Saturday, 21st December, at 8.45 in the evening, and if I am not, the twenty thousand pounds now in my bank will belong to you gentlemen.'

Seven o'clock struck as he was speaking, and the others advised him to hurry off immediately and get ready for his journey. But he said there was no need for him to leave them just yet, as he was always ready; and so it was 7.25 before he said goodbye and left the club.

Twenty-five minutes later he opened the door of his house and found Passepartout waiting for him.

Passepartout was feeling very happy. He had been examining the house, and the things in it, and had noticed its strict organization. Everything showed that his master was a man who lived a quiet and regular life. It was clear that he never went away on journeys, and never went hunting or shooting.

'This will suit me perfectly,' he said to himself. 'I have had many years of change and adventure, and I ask for nothing better than to lead a quiet and regular life with my new master. Excellent!'

Just then his master came in.

'We must leave in ten minutes for Dover and Calais,' said Phileas Fogg. 'We have only eighty days in which to go round the world, so we must not waste any time.'

The calmness with which he gave this information to his servant left that good Frenchman almost breathless with surprise.

'Round the world?'

'Yes, round the world.'

'In eighty days?'

'In eighty days.'

'Leaving in ten minutes' time?'

'Exactly.'

'But what about the things we are to take with us? What about packing?'

'We will take nothing with us except our night clothes. Everything else we shall buy on the way.'

By eight o'clock Passepartout had done the few things that were to be done: he had packed a small travelling bag, and had locked up the rooms. Into the bag Mr Fogg put a large packet of bank notes; he then told his servant to take care of the bag, as there were twenty thousand pounds in it.

They locked the front door, crossed the street, hired a carriage, and drove quickly to Charing Cross Station. At the station the five members of the Reform Club were waiting to see Phileas Fogg leave. He explained to them that he had a passport which he would ask officials to sign at every important place on his journey, to prove that he had been there.

At 8.45 the train began to move; the journey around the world had begun.

Chapter 2   Fix, the Detective

Seven days later, while a small crowd was waiting at Suez for the steamer *Mongolia* to arrive, two men were having a serious talk. One was the British consul, and the other was a thin, impatient little man whose eyes seemed never at rest. This second man was Mr Fix, one of the many detectives sent out to the chief ports in an attempt to catch the bank robber of whom Mr Fogg and his friends had been talking.

Mr Fix had the idea that the robber might have chosen a new way of travelling to America and, instead of crossing the Atlantic, might be going eastwards by way of India and Japan, and so escape being discovered.

The *Mongolia* would only stop for a short time at Suez and would then go on to Bombay. As the passengers came off the boat, they were all watched very carefully by the detective. One of those passengers was Passepartout, who had been sent by his master to get the passport signed by the consul. He went up to Fix and, showing him the passport, explained that he wanted to find the consul. Fix took it and examined it closely. As he read on it the description of Mr Fogg, he became certain that it was the passport of the man he was trying to catch.

'This passport is not yours, is it?' he asked.

'No,' said the other, 'it belongs to my master.'

'Where is your master?' asked Fix.

'On the ship,' answered Passepartout.

'But he must go himself to the consul's office if he wants the passport to be signed by the consul. He cannot send anybody else.'

'Is that so?'

'Certainly.'

'And where is the office?' asked Passepartout.

'Over there,' said the detective, pointing.

'Then I will go and inform my master,' said Passepartout, 'but he won't like having to come himself.'

While Passepartout went back to the boat, the detective walked quickly to the consul's office, and told the consul what he thought.

'I am sure,' he said, 'that the man I am looking for is on board the *Mongolia*.'

'Very well, Mr Fix,' answered the consul. 'I would rather like to see him myself. But if he is, as you suppose, the robber, I don't think that he will come to my office. A thief does not like to show himself and talk about his business. Besides, passengers need not show their passports if they don't want to.'

'But,' said Fix, 'he must not be allowed to go on to India. I must keep him here until I receive from London the warrant for his arrest.'

'I can't help you,' said the consul. 'If the man's passport is in order, I cannot stop him from going on to India.'

At that moment two men came into the office. One was Passepartout and the other was Mr Fogg. Mr Fogg held out the passport and asked the consul to sign it.

The consul read it carefully, and then said: 'You are Mr Phileas Fogg?'

'I am.'

'And this man is your servant?'

'Yes.'

'You have come from London?'

'Yes.'

'And you are going . . . ?'

'To Bombay.'

'Very well, sir. You know that there is no need for you to bring this passport here for my signature.'

'I know that,' answered Mr Fogg, 'but I wish to prove, by your signature, that I have passed through Suez.'

'Very well,' said the consul, and signed the passport.

A few minutes later Fix found Passepartout alone.

'Well, did you get what you wanted?'

'Oh, it's you, is it, sir? Yes, everything is all right. So this is Suez, and we are in Egypt.'

'Just so.'

'In Africa, I believe.'

'Yes, in Africa.'

'I wish I could stay longer, and see something of Africa. But we are travelling so quickly that there's no time for me to stop and see all these interesting places.'

'Are you in such a hurry, then?' asked Fix.

'No, but my master is. He is in a terrible hurry. We left London so suddenly that we did not even have time to pack things for our journey.'

'I can take you to a place where you can buy everything you need,' offered Fix.

'You are really very kind,' answered Passepartout.

As they walked along, the Frenchman said: 'Above all, I must not be too late for the boat!'

'You have plenty of time,' answered Fix. 'It's only twelve o'clock.'

Passepartout pulled out his watch. 'Twelve o'clock,' he said. 'You are joking. It is only eight minutes to ten.'

'Your watch is slow,' answered Fix.

'Slow? My watch? The watch that belonged to my father's grandfather? My watch that is never wrong? Impossible!'

'I see what is the matter,' answered Fix. 'You have kept it at London time, which is about two hours earlier than Suez time. You will have to put it right.'

'Put it right!' cried Passepartout. 'But it isn't wrong!'

'Well, if you don't put the watch right, it will not agree with the sun.'

'So much the worse for the sun, then, sir. The sun may be wrong, but not my watch.'

There was a short silence. Then Fix said, 'Let me see, you were saying that you left London in a hurry.'

'We certainly did. On Wednesday evening Mr Fogg came back from his club much earlier than usual, and three-quarters of an hour later, we had started on our journey.'

'But where is your master going?'

'He is going round the world.'

'Going round the world?' cried Fix.

'Yes, in eighty days. A bet, he says it is, but, between ourselves, I don't believe it. There's something about it that I don't understand.'

'He seems to be a strange man.'

'He certainly is.'

'Is he rich?'

'He must be, and he is taking a lot of money with him, all in new bank notes. And he is spending his money, too, I can tell you.'

'Have you known your master a long time?'

'I had never met him until the day we started. That was the day when I became his servant.'

It is easy to imagine what effect this conversation had on the mind of the detective, who was already certain that Mr Fogg was the bank robber. This sudden journey such a short time after the robbery; this anxiety to reach distant countries, with the excuse of a strange bet – all this persuaded Fix that he was right. He encouraged the Frenchman to say more, and so learned that the servant knew nothing of his master, that Mr Fogg lived alone in London, that he was known to be rich, that nobody knew where his fortune came from, that he was a man who never spoke about himself or his business. Fix discovered, too, that he was in fact going on to Bombay.

'Is Bombay far?' asked Passepartout.

'Yes, quite far,' answered Fix. 'It will take about another ten days of sailing.'

'And where is Bombay?'

'In India.'

'In Asia?'

'Of course.'

◆

Fix went to the consul shortly after this talk. 'I am now quite certain,' he said, 'that I have got him. He pretends to be trying to win a strange bet by going round the world in eighty days.'

'Then he's very clever,' said the consul. 'He expects to get back safely to London after having escaped from the police all over the world.'

'We shall see,' answered Fix.

'You are sure that you are not mistaken?'

'Quite sure.'

'Then why was he so anxious for me to sign his passport?'

'That's what I don't know,' replied the detective. 'But listen to this.' And then in a few words he told the consul what he had learned from Passepartout.

'Yes, it really does seem that he is the man you want,' agreed the consul. 'What are you going to do?'

'Send a telegram to London, telling the people there to send a warrant for his arrest to me at Bombay. Then I shall go on board the *Mongolia*, follow the thief to India, and there go up to him politely with the warrant in my hand and put my hand on his shoulder.'

Fix said goodbye to the consul, sent the telegram, and boarded the *Mongolia*. Shortly after that the steamer made its way through the Red Sea towards India.

◆

Most of the passengers who had joined the *Mongolia* at Brindisi were not going further than India. Some were going to Bombay; others to Calcutta, but by way of Bombay, because a railway had now been built that ran across the country from west to east, so there was no need to make the long sea journey by way of Ceylon.

The day after the boat left Suez, Passepartout happened to see Fix.

'If I am not mistaken, sir,' said he with a smile, 'you are the one who so kindly directed me at Suez.'

'Yes, of course, and you are the servant of that strange Englishman.'

'Just so, Mr . . .'

'Fix.'

'Mr Fix, I am pleased to find you on board. Where are you going?'

'Like you, to Bombay.'

'That's excellent. Have you ever been there before?'

'Well . . . yes . . .' answered Fix, who did not want to say too much.

'Is India an interesting place?' asked Passepartout.

'Very interesting. There are all sorts of lovely things to be seen there. I hope you will have plenty of time to see the country.'

'I hope so too, Mr Fix. After all, it's a foolish thing to spend one's life jumping from a ship to a railway and from a railway to a ship, simply in order to go round the world in eighty days. No, all that sort of thing will come to an end at Bombay, I feel sure.'

'And is Mr Fogg well?' asked Fix, without seeming to be very interested.

'Very well,' answered Passepartout, 'and so am I. I eat enough for three men. It's the sea air that makes me so hungry.'

'I never see your master walking around the ship.'

'No, he doesn't like mixing with other people.'

'Have you considered, Mr Passepartout, that this journey round the world in eighty days might be an excuse for something else, some secret purpose?'

'Well, Mr Fix, I don't know, and what is more, I don't want to know.'

This was the first of many similar conversations between Passepartout and Fix, as the detective thought it wise to make friends with the servant of the man he was following; it might one day be useful.

At Aden, Fogg went on shore to have his passport signed. Passepartout went too, as he never wasted an opportunity to see all that was to be seen.

'Very interesting,' he said to himself; 'if you are looking for new experiences, there is no better way than by travelling.'

On Sunday, 20th October India came in sight.

Chapter 3   The Train to Allahabad

The ship reached Bombay two days earlier than had been expected. At half past four in the afternoon the travellers went on shore, and the train for Calcutta was going to leave at eight o'clock.

Mr Fogg, as you may imagine, went to the passport office, while Mr Fix went, as you may imagine, to the police station, where he asked anxiously whether the warrant had come.

It had not come. Fix was disappointed. He asked the chief of the Bombay police to give him the necessary documents to arrest Mr Fogg. The chief said no – it was a matter for the London police, and not his business at all. There was nothing to be done. Fix was fairly certain that Mr Fogg would go no further than Bombay. So he would arrest the man when the warrant from London finally arrived.

But by this time Passepartout knew that the journey was not at an end. His master had told him that they would leave for Calcutta by the evening train, and so he began to think that, after all, the story of the bet was true, and that they were really going round the world.

He went for a walk in the streets of Bombay, since he liked to see all there was to be seen. Unfortunately for him and his master, though, his wish to see everything resulted in serious trouble.

This is what happened. While making his way towards the station, Passepartout came to the great temple of Malabar Hill. The outside of it looked so fine that he decided to go and admire it from the inside. Now, there were two things that our sightseeing Frenchman did not know. One of them was this – that foreigners are not allowed to go inside Indian temples. The other was that even the Indians themselves are not allowed to enter a temple with their shoes on; they must take their shoes off and leave them outside the door.

Passepartout went in, and he did not take his shoes off. While he was admiring the temple from the inside, three priests threw themselves on him, pulled his shoes off and began to give him a good beating. Passepartout, strong and active, was easily able to get up, knock them down, fight his way out of the temple and run. At five minutes to eight, only a few minutes before the train left, and without his hat or shoes, he reached the railway station.

Fix was there. He had followed Mr Fogg and discovered that he was going to leave the town. He decided immediately that he must follow him to Calcutta, and even further, if necessary. Passepartout did not notice the detective, but Fix heard the explanations that he gave to his master and the story of his adventure.

'Don't let that happen again,' said Phileas Fogg to his servant, as they took their places in the railway carriage.

Fix was just about to board the train himself when a better

plan came into his mind. 'No, I will stay here,' he said to himself. 'Laws have now been broken here in India. I know what to do. I have got my man!'

◆

Mr Fogg and Passepartout were not the only people in the railway carriage; there was a third traveller with them. This was Sir Francis Cromarty, an officer of the Indian Army, who was on his way to Benares.

On Tuesday morning, 22nd October, Sir Francis happened to ask Passepartout the time.

Passepartout pulled out his watch and said, 'Three o'clock.'

'Impossible,' said Sir Francis. 'It must be seven o'clock at least.'

'My watch is never wrong,' replied Passepartout.

Sir Francis tried to make him understand that as they were going towards the east the days became shorter, and each degree that they passed made a difference of four minutes.

But Passepartout could not understand. His watch must be right, he said, and the sun must be wrong. His watch said that it was three o'clock and so it could not be seven o'clock.

As Sir Francis Cromarty became more and more friendly with his travelling companions, it was not long before he learned the reason for their journey. He became most interested, and listened with the greatest care to what Mr Fogg told him.

'You will be very fortunate, Mr Fogg,' he said, 'if you succeed in getting round the world in eighty days. All sorts of things may happen that will delay you. An accident; unexpected problems . . .'

'No,' answered Mr Fogg, 'in spite of accidents and unexpected problems, I am certain to succeed.'

'For example,' answered Sir Francis, 'this adventure of your servant at Bombay. You have no idea how severe the British government is in such matters. Your servant may be arrested and punished.'

'If my servant is arrested and punished for going into a temple without taking his shoes off, it is his business and not mine. If he is stopped at Calcutta and put into prison, I shall, of course, be sorry. But it will not stop me from continuing with my journey.'

'But other things may happen that will delay you,' answered Sir Francis.

At that moment the train came to a stop, and a voice called: 'All passengers get down here!'

Passepartout jumped out of the train to see what the matter was. In a few minutes he came back saying, 'This is the end of the railway!'

'What do you mean?' asked Sir Francis.

'I mean that the train can go no further.'

The passengers got off the train.

'Where are we?' Sir Francis asked a railway official.

'We are at the village of Kholby.'

'Why are we stopping?'

'This is where the railway line comes to an end.'

'How's that?'

'It is not yet completed. The fifty miles of line between here and Allahabad have not yet been built.'

'But the newspapers say that the line is complete.'

'I can't help that,' answered the official. 'The newspapers have made a mistake.'

'But we have paid for the journey from Bombay to Calcutta!' said Sir Francis.

'But the passengers know that they must find some way of their own to get from here to Allahabad.'

Sir Francis was very angry, and Passepartout was ready to fight the railway official.

'Sir Francis,' said Mr Fogg calmly, 'we had better find another way of getting to Allahabad.'

'Mr Fogg, this is going to put an end to your plan.'

17

'Not at all, Sir Francis. I had expected it.'

'What! You knew that the railway was not yet complete?'

'No, but I knew something or other of this sort was certain to happen. This is not serious; I am two days early. There is a ship that leaves Calcutta for Hong Kong at twelve o'clock on the 25th; this is only the 22nd, and we shall get to Calcutta in time.'

It was only too true that the railway ended at this point. The newspapers were mistaken – as they often are. Most of the passengers had known that the line stopped there, and had already hired carriages and horses; so when Mr Fogg and Sir Francis went to find some way of getting to Allahabad, everything had been taken.

'I shall walk,' said Phileas Fogg.

But Passepartout had been more fortunate. 'I think I have found a way,' he said.

'And what's that?'

'An elephant. It belongs to an Indian who lives close by.'

'Let's go and see the elephant,' said Mr Fogg.

Five minutes later the three travellers reached a hut, inside which was an Indian and outside which was an elephant.

Mr Fogg asked if he could hire the animal. The Indian said no. Fogg asked him again and offered the very high price of ten pounds an hour. The answer was no. Twenty pounds? No. Forty pounds? No. Passepartout gave a jump every time the price went up. If it took fifteen hours to get to Allahabad, the Indian would receive six hundred pounds.

Phileas Fogg, without showing any signs of impatience, offered to buy the elephant, and suggested a thousand pounds as the price. The Indian did not want to sell.

Sir Francis Cromarty took Mr Fogg on one side and advised him to think the matter over before going any further. Mr Fogg said that he never thought things over; he always decided things immediately. He had to win a bet of twenty thousand pounds, and to win it he must have the elephant, even if he paid twenty times the value of the animal.

Mr Fogg went back to the Indian. It was easy to see by the look on the man's face that the whole thing was a question of money. Phileas Fogg offered twelve hundred pounds, then fifteen hundred, then eighteen hundred, and at last two thousand pounds.

Then the Indian said he would sell.

The next thing was to find a guide. This was easier. A young Indian, with a pleasant-looking face, offered his services. Mr Fogg promised him a good reward, which made his face look even more pleasant. The Indian knew his business. He fitted a seating arrangement onto the elephant, with a chair on each side.

Mr Fogg paid the Indian in bank notes, which he took from his bag. This made Passepartout feel almost ill. Then Mr Fogg offered to take Sir Francis Cromarty with him to Allahabad, and his offer was accepted. Food was bought in the village. Sir Francis took his place on one of the chairs, and Phileas Fogg on the other. The Indian took his place on the neck of the elephant, and Passepartout sat at the back.

They started at nine o'clock in the morning and, leaving the village, took a path that ran through the forest. They travelled all through the day, and by eight o'clock in the evening they had already got halfway to Allahabad. They started off at six o'clock the next morning, and their guide said that they would reach Allahabad that evening.

At about four o'clock in the afternoon, when they were in the middle of a thick forest, they suddenly heard strange noises – the crying of many voices, and the sound of wild music. The guide stopped, and his face showed his anxiety. He jumped down, tied the elephant to a tree, and then went quietly into the forest. A few moments later he came back, saying, 'We must not be seen! Let us hide; there is danger.' He untied the elephant, and led it to a place from which the travellers could not be seen.

The noises came nearer and nearer. The travellers watched, not knowing what they were going to witness. Then a crowd of priests came into view, half walking and half dancing, half shouting and half singing. Others came behind them pulling a sort of platform on wheels. On this was seated a figure in the shape of a large man or woman with four arms, painted in violent colours.

Sir Francis knew what it was. 'It is the Goddess Kali, the Goddess of Love and Death,' he said.

'The Goddess of Death, perhaps,' said Passepartout, 'but the Goddess of Love – that I can never believe. What an ugly woman!'

The Indian made a sign to him to keep quiet.

Behind this some priests were pulling along a woman, who seemed hardly able to walk. She was young, and very beautiful. Then came another group of priests carrying a dead body. The body was dressed in the fine clothes of an Indian prince.

Chapter 4   A Suttee

Sir Francis looked at all this very sadly and, turning towards the Indian, asked, 'A *suttee*?'

The Indian answered yes.

When the priests had all passed, and their cries could no longer be heard, Mr Fogg turned to Sir Francis and asked him the meaning of the word 'suttee'.

'A "suttee",' he answered, 'is an offering to the gods of the body of a woman whose husband has died. This poor woman will be burned tomorrow morning when the sun rises.'

'Oh! What evil people!' cried Passepartout.

'And the dead body?' Mr Fogg asked.

'The dead body is that of her husband, the prince,' answered their guide.

'In most of India,' explained Sir Francis Cromarty, 'this sort of thing has been stopped. But we can do nothing about it in the wilder parts.'

'The poor girl!' cried Passepartout. 'To be burned alive!'

'Yes,' said Sir Francis, 'burnt alive, and if she were not, you would hardly believe what cruelties she would suffer. They would cut off her hair; they would give her almost nothing to eat; people would treat her worse than a dog. So many of these unfortunate women prefer to be burned than to lead such a terrible life. And there are in fact cases in which the woman offers herself freely. I remember one such case when a young woman asked to be burned with the body of her husband. The governor of course would not allow it. So the woman left the town and went to an area governed by one of the Indian princes, and there she was able to die in the way she wished.'

The guide, who had been listening, said, 'The woman we saw just now, though, is not going to her death because she wants to; she is being forced to do so.'

'She does not seem to be making any effort to escape,' said Sir Francis.

The Indian answered, 'They have made her drink or smoke something that has made her sleepy. She does not know what is happening.'

'But how do you know,' asked Sir Francis, 'that she is being forced to go?'

'Everybody round here knows the story,' answered the man. 'She is a girl of great beauty, the daughter of a rich Bombay trader. Her name is Aouda. Her father and mother died when she was young, and she was forced to marry this old prince. Three months later he died. Knowing what would happen to her, she escaped, but was soon caught. The brother of the prince will get

21

the prince's fortune if this girl dies, and so he has arranged for her to be put to death.'

'Where are they taking her?' asked Mr Fogg.

'To the Pillaji temple, two miles from here. She will spend the night there waiting for the moment when she is to be burned.'

Just as they were going to start their journey again, Mr Fogg turned to Sir Francis and suggested: 'Let us save this woman.'

'Save this woman, Mr Fogg?' cried Sir Francis.

'I am still twelve hours early,' he answered, 'and I can give those twelve hours to her.'

'Mr Fogg, you have a very kind heart!'

'Sometimes – when I have time,' answered Mr Fogg, simply.

They decided to go as near to the temple as possible, and half an hour later they came to a stop among some thick trees. There they talked about the best plan for saving the girl. The Indian knew this temple, and said that the girl was inside it. Would it be possible to go in and take her away while the priests were asleep? Would it be possible to make a hole in the wall? Such things could not be decided until the right moment. But there was no doubt in their minds that if she could be saved, she must be carried off during the night, and not at the moment when she was being taken to the place of her death, for then no man could save her.

◆

Mr Fogg and his companions waited for night to fall. When it got dark, at about six o'clock, they decided to go as far as the temple to see what could be done. By that time, no more noise was heard. The Indians must have been drinking or smoking something that had put them into a deep sleep, so it would perhaps be possible to enter the temple without being noticed.

The guide went first, and the others followed. Before long they came to the edge of a stream, and there they saw in front of them

22

a pile of wood which had been built up by the Indians. On this pile of wood lay the body of the prince, which was to be burned at the same time as the girl whom they were trying to save. A few hundred feet on the other side of this was the temple.

'Follow me,' said the guide, in a low voice.

Soon they came to a place where the ground was covered with sleeping Indians. But to their disappointment, they also saw men who were not asleep and who were on guard, walking up and down in front of the doors of the temple. The travellers supposed that there must be men on guard inside, too.

The Indian went no further. He saw the impossibility of getting into the temple through its entrance, and he went back to his companions. Phileas Fogg and Sir Francis Cromarty understood as well as he did that nothing could be done from that direction, and they talked over the matter in low voices.

'Let us wait,' said Sir Francis. 'It is only eight o'clock, and perhaps these men will go to sleep too, later.'

'Perhaps they will,' said Passepartout.

So Phileas Fogg and his companions lay down at the foot of a tree and waited. Time seemed to pass very slowly. The Indian left them now and again to see what was happening.

At midnight the priests were still on guard. It was clear that they did not intend to sleep. There was only one thing to be done, and that was to make a hole in the wall of the temple. But the question was: would the men inside the temple be watching the girl as carefully as those outside?

After one final discussion, the Indian said that he was ready to start. The others followed him.

Half an hour later they reached the back of the temple without having met anyone. There was no one on guard on this side, where there were neither doors nor windows.

It was a dark night. The moon was low down in the sky and almost covered with clouds. The thick trees made it even darker.

But it was one thing to get to the wall of the temple, and another to get inside it. To do this, Phileas Fogg and his companions had nothing except their pocket knives. Fortunately the wall was made mainly of wood.

They went to work, making as little noise as possible. The Indian and Passepartout made an opening. Suddenly they heard a cry from inside the temple, and at the same time another cry could be heard from outside.

The workers stopped. What had happened? Had their work been noticed? They went back to their hiding place among the trees and waited. Some time passed. Then they saw that men were now guarding the back of the temple in which the young girl was sleeping.

Chapter 5   Saving Aouda

It is difficult to describe the disappointment of the four men. They had got so near to the woman that they wished to save, but they could not save her. They had failed in their efforts. Sir Francis was biting his fingers. Passepartout was in a state of terrible anger and the Indian had some difficulty in keeping him quiet. Fogg, though, showed no feelings at all; he was as calm as ever.

'The only thing that we can do now is to go away,' said Sir Francis, in a low voice.

'We must go away: that is all that we can do,' agreed the Indian.

Passepartout said nothing.

'Let us wait,' said Phileas Fogg. 'I need not get to Allahabad before midday tomorrow.'

'But what are you hoping for?' asked Sir Francis. 'In a few hours daylight will come and then . . .'

'The chance that we are hoping for may come at the last

moment,' answered Fogg.

Sir Francis wondered what Fogg was thinking. What could this cold Englishman possibly be planning to do? Was he going to rush up to the young woman and carry her off at the moment when the Indians were going to burn her? To try to do that would be crazy. But Phileas Fogg was not crazy, so Sir Francis decided to trust him and to wait.

The young Indian did not let his companions stay so close to the temple, but made them come back to the safer place among the trees from where they could see everything but not be seen themselves.

But Passepartout, sitting on the lowest branches of a tree, had an idea, and he began to make a plan. At first he thought, 'What a stupid plan! It cannot succeed.' But later he thought, 'Why not, after all? It's a chance, perhaps the only one!' So then he began to make his way as silently as possible out along the low branches of the tree, the ends of which bent down towards the ground.

The hours went by, and at last there were signs that the sun would soon rise. The moment had come. The sleeping men woke up; the singing and crying started again. The poor girl was now going to die.

The temple doors opened. Mr Fogg and Sir Francis Cromarty could see her as two priests carried her out. For a second it looked as if she were going to make an effort to escape, but a moment later she fell back into the state of sleep caused by whatever they had forced her to take. The crowd of Indians went forward towards the pile of wood. Phileas Fogg and his companions followed. Two minutes later they reached a little stream, not fifty steps away from the pile on which the dead body of the prince lay. They could see the young woman lying beside him.

Oil had been thrown on the wood to make it burn easily. The priests brought fire, and a moment later the wood began to burn.

25

At that moment Sir Francis and the guide held back Mr Fogg, who was just about to jump forward towards the fire. He pushed them away... and at that point the whole scene changed. Cries of terror were heard, as all the Indians threw themselves on the ground.

The old prince was not dead, after all. He was seen to stand up suddenly, to pick up the young woman in his arms and to come down from the pile of wood, carrying her out of the clouds of smoke.

The priests and others turned their faces to the ground: they did not dare to look at the terrible sight. Mr Fogg and Sir Francis were in a state of the greatest surprise. The Indian's mouth hung open, and Passepartout must surely have been equally surprised.

Carrying the girl in his arms, the man who had come to life again walked quickly towards the travellers, and said, 'Let's go!'

It was Passepartout himself! During the night he had slipped off the branch and, unnoticed by the Indians, had climbed onto the pile of wood. There in the darkness he had put on the long golden coat which he took from the dead body of the prince, and had lain down beside the body. In this way, when the right moment came, he was able to do what has just been described.

Acting with the greatest daring, he was fortunate enough to succeed. A moment later the four men disappeared into the forest, the elephant carrying them away as fast as it could go.

But the cries and shouts behind them told them that the trick had been discovered. For on the pile of burning wood the real body of the old prince could now be clearly seen. The priests were returning to their senses and realizing that the young woman had been carried off. They tried to follow and to catch the travellers, but they were too late.

An hour later Passepartout was still laughing over his success. Sir Francis had taken the brave man by the hand. His master had said 'Well done', which, from him, was very high praise.

Passepartout answered that all the honour of the affair belonged to his master. He could only see the funny part of the business, and laughed to think that he had been the dead husband of a beautiful woman: an old Indian prince!

As for the girl, she had no idea of what had happened. She was still asleep.

The elephant moved quickly through the forest, and an hour after leaving the temple the travellers came to a stretch of flat country. At seven o'clock they stopped to rest. The young woman was still in the same state, but Sir Francis had no anxiety about her condition; he knew that in a few hours she would come to her senses and be all right. What he was afraid of was her future. He told Mr Fogg that if Aouda stayed in India, she would certainly, in the end, be caught again by those who wanted to kill her. She would be safe only when she was out of the country.

Phileas Fogg answered that he would give the matter serious consideration.

At ten o'clock they reached Allahabad. From this point the railway started again, and trains ran in less than twenty-four hours from here to Calcutta. Phileas Fogg should, then, get to Calcutta in time to catch the boat that left there the next day, 25th October, at midday, for Hong Kong.

Mr Fogg found a room at the station for the young woman to rest in, and sent Passepartout to buy the clothes and other things that she would need. By the time the servant got back to the station, having enjoyed as many of the sights as possible along the way, Aouda was already much better. She was now awake, and understood, more or less, what had happened. She was certainly beautiful. She spoke English perfectly, and was in every way a lovely and educated woman.

Chapter 6 Stopped by the Police

The train was just about to leave Allahabad Station, and the Indian guide was waiting for his wages. Mr Fogg gave him the money he had promised, and no more, which rather surprised Passepartout, who knew how helpful the man had been. In fact, if the priests of the Pillaji temple later came to hear how he had helped in carrying off the woman that they were going to burn, they would never forgive him, and his life would be in danger. Then there was the question of the elephant. What was to be done with this animal that had been bought at such a high price?

But Phileas Fogg had already come to a decision. He turned to the Indian and said: 'You have been useful and kind. I have paid you for your service but not for your honesty and loyalty. Do you want this elephant? If so, it is yours.'

'You are giving me a fortune!' the man cried in answer.

'Take it, and even then I shall feel that I owe you something.'

'Excellent!' cried Passepartout. 'Take it, my friend. It is your reward!'

◆

A few minutes later, Phileas Fogg, Sir Francis Cromarty and Passepartout, together with Aouda, were in a comfortable railway carriage making their way towards Benares. This town was eighty miles away from Allahabad, but they reached it in two hours.

During this journey the young woman returned completely to her health and senses. It may be better imagined than described how surprised she was to find herself dressed in European clothes, in a comfortable railway carriage, among companions who were total strangers to her! Sir Francis Cromarty told her the story of how she had been saved. He spoke of the great kindness of Phileas Fogg, who had put his life in danger to save her, and of how the daring plan of Passepartout had succeeded.

In answer to these praises Mr Fogg said nothing, and Passepartout said simply, 'Oh, it's not worth talking about!'

Aouda thanked those who had saved her, more by her tears than by her words. Then, as she thought of the terrible time through which she had passed, and of the continuing danger she faced in India, she was frightened.

Phileas Fogg understood what she was thinking, and to put her mind at rest and comfort her, offered – in his coldest manner – to take her to Hong Kong, where she could stay until everything had been forgotten. Aouda accepted the offer gratefully. By chance one of her uncles lived there and was one of the chief traders of that small British island.

At half past twelve the train stopped at Benares. Here Sir Francis Cromarty left them, after wishing them every success on their journey.

'I hope that you reach London in time to win your bet,' he said.

Aouda said that she would never forget how much he had helped in saving her from a terrible death. Passepartout shook hands with him with such force that Sir Francis almost cried out in pain. Mr Fogg touched his hand lightly, and said, 'Thank you.'

The train continued towards Calcutta, and arrived there the next morning at seven o'clock. The boat did not leave until midday, and so Mr Fogg was five hours early.

As the travellers were leaving the station, a policeman came up to their leader and said: 'Mr Phileas Fogg?'

'Yes,' he answered, 'that is my name.'

'Is this man your servant?' asked the policeman.

'Yes.'

'Please follow me, both of you.'

Mr Fogg made no movement of surprise. The policeman was an officer of the law, and for every Englishman the law is something to be obeyed. Passepartout, being a Frenchman, tried to argue. But the policeman tapped him with his stick, and Phileas Fogg ordered him to obey.

'May this young lady come with us?' asked Mr Fogg.

'She may,' answered the policeman.

The policeman led them towards a four-wheeled carriage with two horses. They got in and drove off. Nobody spoke during the journey, which lasted about twenty minutes.

At the police station they were taken into a room and told that they would be brought before a judge at half past eight. The policeman then left them, locking the door behind him.

'Well, we're caught!' cried Passepartout.

Aouda turned to Mr Fogg, saying, 'You must leave me! It is because of me that the police have taken you! It is because you saved me!'

Fogg answered simply that that was not possible. To be brought before a judge for having saved a woman from those who were going to burn her? Impossible. There must be a mistake. Mr Fogg added that in any case he would not leave Aouda behind, and that he would take her with him to Hong Kong.

'But the boat leaves at twelve o'clock!' said Passepartout.

'Before twelve o'clock we shall be on board the boat,' answered Mr Fogg.

He said it so seriously and naturally that Passepartout could not help saying to himself, 'Yes, of course, that is certain. Before twelve o'clock we shall be on board.'

At half past eight the door opened. The policeman came in and then took the prisoners to the courtroom. The judge appeared a few moments later, and sat down.

'Call the first case,' he said.

'Phileas Fogg!' called out an officer.

'I am here,' answered Fogg.

'Passepartout!'

'I am here!' answered Passepartout.

'Very well,' said the judge. 'For the last two days we have been watching the trains from Bombay.'

'But why?' asked Passepartout. 'What have we done?'

'You will see,' said the judge. 'Call the priests.'

The door was opened, and three Indian priests came into the hall.

'That's what it is!' said Passepartout to himself. 'Those are the ones who were going to burn our young lady!'

The priests stood in front of the judge, while the official read out the complaint – that Phileas Fogg and his servant had broken the law by behaving in a violent and disorderly way while on land which formed part of a temple.

'You have heard the complaint?' asked the judge.

'I have,' answered Mr Fogg, looking at his watch.

'Is it true?'

'Yes, it is true, and I am waiting to hear those priests tell you what they were going to do at the Pillaji temple when we stopped them.'

The priests looked at each other in surprise. They seemed not to understand what Fogg had said.

'Yes!' cried Passepartout impatiently. 'At the temple of Pillaji, where they were going to burn the poor girl!'

The priests looked more and more surprised, and the judge was totally confused.

'Burn who?' asked the judge. 'Who were they going to burn in the middle of the town of Bombay?'

'Bombay?' cried Passepartout.

'Yes, of course. We know nothing about the temple of Pillaji; we are talking about the temple of Malabar Hill, in Bombay.'

'And in proof,' added the official, 'here are the shoes.' And he held up the shoes.

'My shoes!' cried Passepartout.

Phileas Fogg and his servant had quite forgotten what had

happened at the temple in Bombay, but it was this that was the cause of their being brought in front of the judge in Calcutta.

Fix had realized immediately how he could make use of the business of the shoes. He had been to the Bombay temple and had advised the priests to make a complaint to the government. If they did this, the man who had gone into the temple with his shoes on, and then knocked down the priests, would be forced to pay them a large sum of money. The priests had agreed, and had come with Fix to Calcutta by the next train.

Because of the time that Fogg and his companions had spent saving the young girl, Fix and the priests had reached Calcutta first. Fix had sent a telegram from Bombay to the Calcutta police, telling them to stop Mr Fogg and Passepartout when they got off the train, so he was very disappointed when he learned that nothing had been seen of them. He then thought that they had got off at one of the stations and were making their way towards the south of India.

For twenty-four hours, suffering from terrible anxiety, he had been watching at the station. That morning his patience had been rewarded when he saw the two men get off the train. He immediately ordered a policeman to stop them and to bring them to court. But who the woman was, and how she had come to join them, was more than he could understand.

If Passepartout had been paying less attention to his own business, he would have seen Mr Fix, sitting in a corner and listening with the greatest interest to everything that was said. For at Calcutta, as at Bombay and Suez, the warrant for Mr Fogg's arrest had not yet reached him.

The judge noted that Passepartout had said that the shoes were his.

'You agree, then,' said the judge, 'that what has been said is true. You were inside the temple and you had not taken off your shoes.'

'Yes,' said Passepartout.

'According to English law,' the judge went on, 'the ideas of the Indians in such matters must be respected. It has been proved that you behaved in a disrespectful and disorderly way in the temple on Malabar Hill, Bombay, on 20th October. For this you will be kept in prison for fourteen days, and you must pay three hundred pounds.'

'Three hundred pounds?' cried Passepartout.

'And,' added the judge, 'although it has not been proved that Phileas Fogg had anything to do with the matter, he is the master of this man, and so must suffer for the fault of his servant. You will be kept in prison for seven days and pay a fine of a hundred and fifty pounds.'

Fix, in his corner, was very happy. The warrant would certainly come before the seven days had passed.

Passepartout was in a terrible state, as may be imagined. His master's plans had failed; the bet would be lost, and so would Mr Fogg's whole fortune. And all because, like a fool, he had gone into that temple.

Mr Fogg showed no sign of disappointment. He said, calmly, 'I offer bail.'

'You have the right to do so,' agreed the judge.

This did not suit Mr Fix at all, but he felt no anxiety when he heard the judge say, 'As Phileas Fogg and his servant are strangers, the amount of bail will be one thousand pounds for each of them.'

'I will pay it,' said Mr Fogg. And out of the bag that Passepartout was carrying he took a packet of bank notes and put it on the table in front of the court official!

'This money will be given back to you when you have served your time in prison,' said the judge. 'For now, you are out on bail.'

'Come along,' said Phileas Fogg to his servant.

'But at least they must give me back my shoes!' cried Passepartout, in an angry voice.

They gave him his shoes.

'They have cost a lot of money,' he said. 'More than a thousand pounds each! And they do not fit very well, either.'

Passepartout, in a very unhappy state of mind, followed Mr Fogg, who had offered his arm to Aouda. Fix still hoped that the robber (as he thought Mr Fogg to be) would never agree to lose the two thousand pounds, and that he would go to prison for seven days. All the same, he followed him closely.

Mr Fogg took a carriage, and Aouda, Passepartout and he took their places in it. Fix ran behind it until they reached the port, where the carriage stopped. Half a mile out to sea was the steamer *Rangoon*. It was eleven o'clock, and Mr Fogg was one hour early.

Fix saw him get down from the carriage and, with his companions, take his place in a boat which set off immediately in the direction of the *Rangoon*. The detective stamped his feet with disappointment.

'He has gone!' he cried. 'And two thousand pounds have gone too! The thief! I will follow him to the end of the world, but at the rate he is spending the money, there will be nothing left of what he has stolen!'

The detective had some reason for thinking this. Mr Fogg had, as a matter of fact, spent more than five thousand pounds since he had left London – and as the money grew less, so also did any reward that the detective could hope for when this affair was over.

Chapter 7   Calcutta to Hong Kong

The *Rangoon* was a fine iron steamship, as fast as the *Mongolia* but not as comfortable. It was, though, only 3,500 miles from Calcutta to Hong Kong – which meant only eleven or twelve days at sea.

Aouda came to know Phileas Fogg much better, and told him how grateful she was to him for having saved her and for taking so much care of her. She told Mr Fogg the story of her life, and spoke about her uncles, who were rich traders, one in Bombay, and the other – whom she was going to join – in Hong Kong. Mr Fogg listened to her in what seemed to be a very cold and distant way, and showed no sign of any friendly feelings towards her. He treated her, of course, with the greatest politeness, but it was the politeness of a machine. He made sure that she had everything she needed for her comfort and came regularly to see her. If he did not talk much, he at least listened to her. Aouda found it difficult to understand his behaviour, but Passepartout explained to her something of his master's ways and habits. He told her, too, the reason for his journey round the world.

The weather was fine and the sea was calm, and the steamer made its way across the Bay of Bengal in the direction of Singapore.

The day before the *Rangoon* reached Singapore, Passepartout suddenly found himself face to face with Mr Fix.

'Mr Fix! What are you doing here? I thought you were in Bombay. Are you travelling round the world, too?'

'Oh, no!' answered Fix. 'I expect to stop at Hong Kong – at least for a few days.'

'But how is it that I haven't seen you on board between Calcutta and here?'

'Oh, I haven't been feeling very well and so stayed in my cabin. And how is your master, Mr Phileas Fogg?'

'He is quite well, thank you, and not a day late in his journey. Ah, Mr Fix; here is something you don't know. We have a young lady with us.'

'A young lady?' said Fix, who looked as if he had no idea what Passepartout meant.

Passepartout then told him the story. He told him about the adventure in Bombay, buying the elephant at the price of two thousand pounds, saving Aouda in the forest, and how they had been stopped at Calcutta.

Fix, who certainly knew the last part of the story, acted as if he knew nothing at all.

'But,' asked Fix, 'does your master mean to take this lady to Europe with him?'

'No, Mr Fix, no. We are simply going to leave her in the care of her uncle, a rich trader in Hong Kong.'

Fix was disappointed. He had thought that this business of the saving of Aouda would give him the chance to make fresh trouble for Mr Fogg at Hong Kong.

'May I offer you something to drink, Mr Passepartout?'

'Thank you; you may,' answered the Frenchman.

After this reunion, the detective and Passepartout met frequently. Fix did not try to get any more information out of his companion and only caught sight of Mr Fogg once or twice as he sat in the cabin talking to Aouda or playing cards.

Passepartout began to wonder very seriously about the strange chance that kept Fix with them. And it really was surprising. Here was this very kind gentleman, whom he met first at Suez, sailing on the *Mongolia*, getting off at Bombay where he was supposed to stay, then appearing on the *Rangoon* on his way to Hong Kong. In fact, here he was following Mr Fogg step by step. It was worth thinking about. It was most strange. Passepartout felt certain that Fix would leave Hong Kong at the same time as Mr Fogg, and probably by the same steamer.

If Passepartout had thought about the matter for a hundred years, he would never have guessed the real reason why his master was being followed. He would never have imagined that Mr Fogg was being chased round the world because he was believed to be a robber. But it is human nature to find an explanation for everything, and Passepartout found an explanation that seemed very reasonable. Fix, he felt sure, had been sent by the members of the Reform Club to see that the journey was carried out fairly and according to the agreement.

'It must be that!' he said to himself, proud at his cleverness. 'He has been sent secretly to make sure that my master is not cheating. That is not right. Ah! Gentlemen of the Reform Club, you will be sorry for this!'

Pleased with his discovery, Passepartout made up his mind, all the same, to say nothing to his master about it, fearing that Mr Fogg's feelings would be hurt by this distrust of his honesty. But he promised himself that he would play some tricks on Mr Fix.

◆

On Wednesday afternoon, 30th October, the *Rangoon* passed through the narrow stretch of water which separates the island of Sumatra from the country of the Malays. Beautiful little islands, with their steep mountain sides, hid the view of Sumatra from the passengers.

At four o'clock the next morning the *Rangoon*, having arrived half a day earlier than usual, stopped at Singapore to take on more coal. Phileas Fogg marked this gain in his notebook and went on shore with Aouda, who wished to go for a short walk. Fix, distrusting every action of Fogg's, followed him secretly. Passepartout was amused to see him doing this, and went on shore to buy some fresh food.

The island of Singapore is neither large nor particularly striking in appearance, since there are no mountains; it is not, though, unattractive. After a pleasant drive of two hours among the woods and hills, Aouda and her companion returned to the town, and at ten o'clock went back on board the boat – followed by the detective, who had, of course, never lost sight of them. Passepartout was waiting for them on the *Rangoon*. He had been buying quantities of the fruits of the country, and offered some to Aouda, who was very grateful for them.

At eleven o'clock the *Rangoon*, having taken on more coal, steamed out of the port, and a few hours later the passengers could see no more of the high mountains and forests of Malacca.

Thirteen hundred miles separate Singapore from Hong Kong, a small British island lying off the coast of China. Phileas Fogg expected to spend no more than six days in getting there, so that he could take the boat that left Hong Kong on 6th November for Yokohama, one of the chief towns of Japan.

The weather, which had been fairly good up to then, changed when the moon entered its last quarter, and the sea became rough. At times there was a strong wind – and fortunately it blew from the south-east, the right direction for the ship. The captain often raised the sails, and with these and the steam the ship went forward at great speed past the coasts of Annam and Cochin China.

The ship still did not go fast enough to please Passepartout, since special care had to be taken in bad weather, which slowed them down. He felt angry with the captain, the engineer and the shipping company. Mr Fogg, on the other hand, showed no impatience or anxiety at all.

'You seem to be in a great hurry to get to Hong Kong,' said Mr Fix to Passepartout one day.

'Yes, in a great hurry,' answered Passepartout.

'You think that Mr Fogg is anxious to catch the boat to Yokohama?'

'Terribly anxious.'

'Then you believe in this journey round the world?'

'I do. Don't you, Mr Fix?'

'No, I don't!'

'You old devil!' answered Passepartout.

This answer made the detective wonder what he meant. He felt rather worried without quite knowing why. Had the Frenchman guessed who he was? He hardly knew what to think. Passepartout could not have guessed his secret, but what he said certainly meant something.

Another day Passepartout went even further. He could not help saying: 'When we get to Hong Kong, Mr Fix, I wonder whether we shall have the misfortune to leave you there?'

'Well,' answered Fix, not quite knowing what to say, 'I hardly know; perhaps . . .'

'Ah!' said Passepartout. 'If you come with us, I shall be very pleased. Come now! As you are a servant of the shipping company, you can hardly leave us during the journey, can you? First you were only going as far as Bombay, and now you will soon be in China! America isn't far, and from America to Europe is only a step!'

Fix looked carefully at Passepartout, on whose face there was a most pleasant smile, and decided to treat what he said as a joke. But Passepartout could not stop, and went on: 'Do you get much money for your sort of work?'

'Yes and no,' answered Fix. 'There are good times and bad. But of course I travel free.'

'Oh, I'm sure you do,' cried Passepartout with a laugh.

After this talk Fix went back to his cabin and began to think. Passepartout had certainly guessed who he was. In some way or other Passepartout had come to know that he was a detective. But had he told his master? What was Passepartout's part in this business? Was he himself one of the bank robbers? Did Passepartout and his master know everything? In that case he,

Fix, had lost the game.

Fix spent several hours worrying, sometimes believing that all was lost and sometimes hoping that Fogg knew nothing of the real state of things. He could not make up his mind how to act for the best.

In the end he decided he would speak openly to Passepartout if he could not manage to arrest Fogg at Hong Kong, and if Fogg was not going to stay on that island. He, Fix, would then tell Passepartout everything. Either the servant was one of the robbers or he was not. If he was, then Fix could not succeed; if he was not, then it would be in Passepartout's interest to help Fix to arrest Fogg.

That is how matters stood between those two men, but what about Fogg and Aouda? Passepartout could not make it out. She was clearly very grateful towards the Englishman, but what were Fogg's feelings towards her? He was certainly ready at all times to protect her, but he was equally certainly not in love with her. And Fogg did not seem to worry at all about his chances of winning or losing the bet; the one who worried continually was Passepartout.

One day he was watching the powerful engines.

'There isn't enough steam,' he cried. 'We are not moving! These Englishmen are afraid of using steam. Ah, if this were an American ship, the engines would perhaps blow up, but we would move faster!'

◆

During the last days of this journey the weather was terrible. The wind blew harder and harder from the north-west — which was the wrong direction. The ship rolled in the rough sea, and the passengers were very uncomfortable.

On 3rd and 4th November the sea was rougher still, and progress was even slower. If the wind did not drop, the ship would be at least twenty hours late. Then it would be too late to catch the steamer to Yokohama. But Phileas Fogg did not seem to be at all worried.

Fix was very pleased. If the *Rangoon* reached Hong Kong after the Yokohama steamer had left, Fogg would have to stay on the island for a few days. So he welcomed the grey sky and the winds. He was rather seasick, it is true, but that did not matter.

But the impatience of Passepartout can easily be imagined. It was impossible for him to stay below. He climbed up the masts and helped with the sails. He jumped from rope to rope and amused the sailors by his acrobatic tricks. He questioned the captain, the officers and the sailors, who could not help laughing at his anxiety. He wanted to know exactly how long the bad weather would last.

Finally the wind died down and blew from the right direction. During the day of 5th November the sea grew calmer. Passepartout grew calmer too, as the ship increased its speed.

But it was impossible to make up for the lost time. There was nothing to be done, and land was not seen until the 6th, at five o'clock in the morning. Phileas Fogg had expected to reach Hong Kong on the 5th. He was twenty-four hours late. He would certainly not be able to catch the steamer for Yokohama.

At six o'clock the pilot came on board the *Rangoon* to help guide the ship into port. Passepartout was most anxious to go and ask him whether the Yokohama steamer had left. But he dared not do so, preferring to hold onto his hopes until the last moment. He had spoken about his fears to Fix, who had tried to comfort him.

'There is nothing to worry about,' he said. 'If your master does not catch the boat for Yokohama, he only has to take the next one.'

This answer had made Passepartout angry.

But if Passepartout dared not question the pilot, Mr Fogg did.

He asked when the next boat would leave Hong Kong for Yokohama.

'Tomorrow morning,' answered the pilot.

'Ah,' said Mr Fogg, without showing any surprise.

Passepartout heard these words, and wanted to throw his arms lovingly round the pilot's neck. Fix heard the answer, too, but he would have preferred to break the pilot's neck.

'What is the name of the steamer?' asked Mr Fogg.

'The *Carnatic*,' answered the pilot.

'But wasn't the *Carnatic* to leave yesterday?'

'Yes, sir, but one of its boilers had to be repaired, and so the boat will not sail until tomorrow.'

'Thank you,' answered Mr Fogg, and went down below.

Passepartout took the pilot's hand and shook it with violence, saying, 'You are a lovely man!'

The pilot probably never knew why Passepartout was so pleased with him; he went calmly on with his duties.

At one o'clock the *Rangoon* tied up, and the passengers landed. It must be said that Phileas Fogg had been extremely fortunate. Without the necessary repair to its boiler, the *Carnatic* would have left Hong Kong the day before, and passengers for Japan would have had to wait a week for the next ship. Mr Fogg was twenty-four hours late, but this would not be a very serious matter. The steamer from Yokohama to San Francisco would have to wait for the *Carnatic* since it connected with the Hong Kong boat, but no doubt it would be easy to make up for the twenty-four hours during the crossing of the Pacific.

Chapter 8   Passepartout Drinks Too Much

The *Carnatic* was expected to leave the next morning at five o'clock. So Mr Fogg had sixteen hours ahead of him during which time he could do his business – that is to say, take Aouda to her uncle and leave her there.

Mr Fogg, the lady, and Passepartout landed and took rooms at the Club Hotel. Leaving Aouda in her room, Fogg went to find the Indian uncle in whose care he would leave her. At the same time he ordered Passepartout to stay at the hotel so that the lady would not be alone.

Mr Fogg paid a visit to one of the chief business houses of the town, where he was certain that the Honourable Mr Jejeeh, Aouda's uncle, would be known. But here he received the information that this rich Indian trader had given up his business two years before. He had made his fortune and had gone to live in Europe – in Holland, it was thought.

Phileas Fogg returned to the Club Hotel. He asked to see Aouda, and told her that her uncle was no longer in Hong Kong and that he had probably gone to live in Holland.

Aouda did not answer immediately. She thought for a few moments and then asked: 'What shall I do, Mr Fogg?'

'It is quite simple. Come to Europe.'

'But I can't give you so much trouble.'

'It is no trouble at all. Passepartout!'

'Yes, sir,' answered his servant.

'Go to the *Carnatic* and ask for three cabins.'

Passepartout went off to do so, very pleased to think that they would not lose the company of the young Indian lady.

At the port he saw Fix walking up and down near the *Carnatic* with a look of disappointment on his face.

'Good!' thought Passepartout to himself. 'Things are not going well for the gentlemen of the Reform Club.'

There was good reason for Fix to be disappointed; the warrant for the arrest of Mr Fogg had not reached Hong Kong. It was certainly on its way, but it would come too late. From Hong Kong onwards Fogg would be outside the reach of English law, and so could not be arrested. If Fix could not keep him in Hong Kong for a few days, he would escape.

Passepartout went up to Fix with a pleasant smile.

'Well, Mr Fix, have you decided to come with us as far as America?'

'Yes,' answered Fix between his teeth.

Passepartout burst out laughing.

'I knew it!' he cried. 'I was certain that you could not bear to separate yourself from us. Come and book a cabin.'

They went into the office of the shipping company and booked cabins for four people. The man at the office pointed out that as the repairs to the *Carnatic* had already been finished, the ship would leave that evening at eight o'clock, and not the next morning, as had been arranged.

'That will suit my master. I will go and warn him,' said Passepartout.

At that moment Fix came to a decision. He would tell Passepartout everything. It was the only way to keep Phileas Fogg in Hong Kong.

On leaving the office, Fix said: 'You have plenty of time. Let's go and have something to drink.'

'Very well,' answered Passepartout, 'but we mustn't stay long.'

They went into a large hall that seemed to be a sort of bar. At one end of the room there was a big bed on which several people were lying asleep. Another thirty or more people were sitting at tables and drinking.

Fix and Passepartout sat down, and Fix ordered two bottles of wine. The Frenchman, finding it to his taste, drank a glass – then two glasses, three, and more. Fix drank little, and watched his companion closely. They discussed a range of subjects, particularly Fix's good idea of joining them on the *Carnatic*. Talking of this steamer made Passepartout remember that he must go and tell his master about the change in the hour of sailing. He got up.

'Wait a moment,' said Fix.

'Well, what is it, Mr Fix?'

'I wish to talk to you about a serious matter.'

'A serious matter!' cried Passepartout, drinking the last of the wine. 'Well, we will talk about it tomorrow. I haven't time today.'

'Wait,' said Fix. 'It's about your master.'

Passepartout looked at Fix and, seeing the strange look on his face, sat down again.

'What have you got to tell me?' asked Passepartout.

Fix laid his hand on his companion's arm and, lowering his voice, said: 'You have guessed who I am?'

'Of course I have!' answered Passepartout, smiling.

'Then I will tell you everything—'

'Now that I know everything! Very good! Go on. But let me first tell you that these gentlemen are spending their money needlessly.'

'Needlessly!' said Fix. 'It is easy to see that you do not know how much money—'

'Yes, I do. Twenty thousand pounds.'

'No, fifty-five thousand pounds,' answered Fix.

'What!' cried Passepartout. 'Well, that is all the more reason why I should not lose a moment,' he added, as he got up again.

'Yes, fifty-five thousand pounds!' answered Fix, forcing Passepartout to sit down by ordering another bottle – this time, though, of a drink much stronger than wine.

'And if I succeed, I shall get a reward of two thousand pounds. And listen to me: if you help me, I will give you half of that. Will you accept a thousand pounds for helping me?'

'Helping you?' cried Passepartout with his eyes very wide open.

'Yes, for helping me to keep Mr Fogg in Hong Kong for a few days.'

'What are you saying?' cried Passepartout. 'What! Is it not

enough to have my master followed, to have doubts about him? And now these gentlemen want to put difficulties in his way! I am ashamed of them!'

'What do you mean? What are you talking about?' asked Fix, who understood nothing of what Passepartout was saying.

'I mean this, that it is dishonesty, pure dishonesty! You might as well take money out of Mr Fogg's pocket!'

'That's just what we are hoping to do!' answered Fix.

'But it's a trick!' cried Passepartout, who had been drinking glass after glass from the new bottle, not noticing in his excitement what he was doing. 'An evil trick! "Gentlemen" they call themselves!'

Fix understood less and less.

'Colleagues!' cried Passepartout. 'Members of the Reform Club! Let me tell you, Mr Fix, that my master is an honest man, and that when he bets he expects to win his bet honestly.'

'But who do you think I am?' asked Fix.

'You?' answered Passepartout. 'Why, you are a man sent by the members of the Reform Club, to keep watch over my master – a piece of work of which they ought to be ashamed! Oh, for some time past I have known who you are, and I have taken good care not to say anything to my master about it!'

'He knows nothing?' asked Fix, coming out of his confusion.

'Nothing,' answered Passepartout, emptying his glass again.

The detective began to think hard. He said nothing for a few moments. What should he do? Passepartout's mistake made the detective's plan more difficult. It was clear that Passepartout was perfectly honest and open; that he had had nothing to do with the robbery.

'Well,' he thought, 'as he has had nothing to do with the robbery, he will help me.'

The detective made up his mind for the second time. Besides, there was no time to be lost. He *must* arrest Fogg in Hong Kong.

'Listen,' said Fix. 'Listen to me carefully. I am not what you think; I have not been sent by the members of the Reform Club.'

'I don't believe you!' said Passepartout.

'I am a detective sent by the London police.'

'You! A London detective!'

'Yes, and I can prove it. Look at my papers.'

He took out his papers and showed them to his companion. The papers were signed by the chief of police. Passepartout looked at them and then at Fix, too surprised to say a word.

'This bet,' said Fix, 'is only a trick. By betting that he could go round the world in eighty days, he made you and the members of the Reform Club help him to escape from the police.'

'Why should he want to escape from the police? What has he done?'

'Listen,' said Fix. 'On 28th September, fifty-five thousand pounds were stolen from the Bank of England. We have a description of the man who stole the money. Here is the description. It is exactly that of your master.'

'Impossible,' cried Passepartout, striking the table. 'My master is the most honest man in the world!'

'How do you know that?' said Fix. 'You don't even know him. You became his servant on the day he left England, and he left in a great hurry, and without any luggage. The only reason he gave for leaving was this foolish bet. And he took with him a very large sum of money. Do you mean to tell me that he is an honest man?'

'Yes, yes, I do,' answered the poor man.

'As you helped him to escape, you will be arrested too.'

Passepartout was holding his head between his hands. His face was quite changed. He dared not look at the detective. What? Phileas Fogg a thief? He, the good man who had so bravely saved Aouda? But in everything else he had acted exactly as a thief would act, and appearances were against him. Passepartout tried not to believe what Fix had said. He refused to think that his master was guilty. But he had drunk so much that it was difficult for him to think clearly.

'Well, what do you want me to do?' he asked the detective at last.

'Listen,' answered Fix. 'I have followed Mr Fogg as far as here, but I have not yet received the warrant for his arrest. So you must help me to prevent him from leaving Hong Kong.'

'Help you to keep him here?'

'Yes, and I will share with you the two thousand pounds promised by the Bank of England.'

'Never!' cried Passepartout, trying to stand up. But he fell back in his chair, feeling both his strength and his reason leaving him.

'Mr Fix,' he said, making every effort to speak. 'Even . . . even if what you tell me is true . . . even if he is the thief . . . the thief you are looking for . . . and I don't think he is a thief . . . I am in his service . . . I have never seen him to be anything but a good and brave man . . . What? Help you to catch him? . . . Never! . . . Not for all the gold in the world . . . I am not the sort of man to do that sort of thing!'

'You refuse?'

'I refuse.'

'All right. Forget that I have said anything to you,' said Fix. 'Drink this; it will do you good.'

Saying this the detective poured a full glass out of the bottle and made the Frenchman drink it.

This was all that was needed to finish Passepartout completely. He fell heavily from his chair and lay on the ground without moving.

'Good,' thought Fix. 'Mr Fogg will not be warned of the changed hour of the sailing of the *Carnatic*, and if he does leave, he will at least leave without the company of this Frenchman!'

Then he paid for the drinks and went out.

Chapter 9 Mr Fogg Misses the Boat

While all this was happening, Mr Fogg and Aouda were out for a walk. Since Aouda had accepted his offer to take her to Europe, he had been thinking of what would be needed for her journey. An Englishman such as he might go round the world with no luggage except a small bag, but a lady could not be expected to do the same. So it was necessary to buy clothes for her, and all sorts of other things needed for travelling. Mr Fogg arranged everything with his usual calmness, and when the young woman said he was being too kind to her, he replied: 'All this is a part of my plan. Please say no more.'

Having bought everything they needed, Mr Fogg and the young woman went back to the hotel, where they were served with an excellent dinner. Then Aouda, who was rather tired, went to her room.

Mr Fogg spent the whole evening reading the newspapers. If he were a man who was ever surprised at anything, he would have been surprised at Passepartout's failure to return. But knowing that the *Carnatic* would not leave Hong Kong until the next morning, he did not worry about his missing servant. The next morning, though, Passepartout did not answer the bell when he rang for him.

Nobody knows what Mr Fogg thought when he was told that his servant had not come back. But he picked up his bag, called Aouda, and ordered a carriage to take them to the port. It was then four o'clock, and the *Carnatic* was going to leave at five.

When the carriage came to the door of the hotel, Mr Fogg and Aouda took their seats in it. Half an hour later they reached the port, and at that point Mr Fogg was informed that the *Carnatic* had left the night before.

Mr Fogg had expected to find both the boat and his servant, and now he had to do without either of them. But no disappointment showed on his face, and when Aouda looked anxiously at him he simply remarked: 'It's nothing. It doesn't matter.'

At that moment somebody who had been watching him came up to Mr Fogg. It was Fix, who said good morning and then asked:

'Were you not one of the passengers on the *Rangoon* that came in yesterday?'

'Yes, sir,' answered Mr Fogg coldly, 'but I have not the honour of knowing you.'

'Excuse me, but I expected to find your servant here.'

'Do you know where he is?' asked the lady.

'What!' answered Fix. 'Isn't he with you?'

'No,' answered Aouda. We have not seen him since yesterday. Has he perhaps sailed on the *Carnatic*?'

'Without you? That is hardly possible,' answered the detective. 'But excuse my question, were you expecting to leave by the *Carnatic*?'

'Yes.'

'I, too, was hoping to leave by it, and I am very disappointed. The *Carnatic*, having completed its repairs, left Hong Kong nine hours earlier than expected without warning anybody, and now we must wait a week for the next steamer.'

As he said the words 'a week', Fix felt that he would burst with joy. Fogg staying a week in Hong Kong. There would be time to receive the warrant. Fortune was at last smiling on the officer of the law.

He did not feel so happy when he heard Phileas Fogg's next words.

'But there must be other ships in the port of Hong Kong.'

Mr Fogg, offering his arm to Aouda, went off to find a ship that might be leaving. Fix followed them. But for once fortune was against Mr Fogg. He searched for hours. He was ready to hire a ship to take them to Yokohama, but he found none. Fix began to hope again.

Mr Fogg did not give up hope. He was about to continue his search, even as far as Macao if necessary, when a sailor came up to him.

'Are you looking for a boat, sir?' he asked.

'You have a boat ready to sail?' asked Mr Fogg.

'Yes, sir.'

'Is it a fast boat?'

'Between eight and nine miles an hour. Would you like to see it?'

'Yes.'

'You shall. Do you want to go for a sail?'

'I want to go to Yokohama.'

The sailor opened his eyes and mouth wide.

'You are joking, sir.'

'No. I have missed the *Carnatic*, and I must be in Yokohama by the 14th at the latest so that I can catch the steamer for San Francisco.'

'I'm sorry,' said the sailor, 'but it's impossible.'

'I'll offer you a hundred pounds a day, and two hundred pounds more if I get there in time.'

'Do you mean it?'

'I mean it.'

The sailor walked off for a few moments to think. He looked at the sea, his feelings torn between the wish to earn such a large sum of money and the fear of going so far in a small boat. Fix waited in a state of the greatest anxiety.

During this time Mr Fogg had turned towards Aouda.

'You will not be afraid?' he asked.

'With you, no, Mr Fogg,' she answered.

The sailor came up to them again.

'Well, Captain?' said Mr Fogg.

'Well, sir, I cannot put my life into danger, nor those of my men, nor yours, on such a long journey in a small boat and at this time of the year. Besides, we shall not get there in time, since it is 1,650 miles from Hong Kong to Yokohama.'

'1,600,' said Mr Fogg.

'It's the same thing.'

Fix breathed again.

'But there may be another way out of the difficulty.'

'And what is that?' asked Phileas Fogg.

'By going to Nagasaki, in the extreme south of Japan, a distance of 1,100 miles, or to Shanghai, which is 800 miles from Hong Kong. By going to Shanghai we would stay close to the coast of China, which would be safer; and besides, the winds blow in that direction this time of the year.'

'Captain,' answered Phileas Fogg, 'I am supposed to take the American steamer at Yokohama, and not at Shanghai or at Nagasaki.'

'But why?' answered the captain. 'The San Francisco steamer does not start from Yokohama. It stops there and at Nagasaki, but it really starts its journey at Shanghai.'

'Are you sure?'

'Quite sure.'

'And when does the steamer leave Shanghai?'

'On the 11th at seven o'clock in the evening. So we have four days ahead of us. Four days, that's ninety-six hours, so that at the speed of eight miles an hour, which is possible with a good wind and if the sea is calm, we can do the 800 miles that separate us from Shanghai.'

'And you can leave . . . ?'

'In an hour. I only need enough time to get the food on board and the sails raised.'

'Very well. I agree. Are you the master of the boat?'

'Yes. John Bunsby, master of the *Tankadere.*'

'Shall I give you some of the money now?'

'If you don't mind.'

'Here are two hundred pounds. Sir,' added Phileas Fogg, turning towards Fix, 'if you would like to join us . . .'

'Sir,' answered Fix, 'I was going to ask you to take me.'

'Very well. In half an hour we shall be on board.'

'But poor Passepartout,' said Aouda, who was very anxious about the disappearance of the servant.

'I will do all I can for him,' answered Phileas Fogg.

And while Fix, in a very bad temper, was heading for the boat, the other two went to the police station of Hong Kong. There Phileas Fogg gave a description of Passepartout and left enough money to send him back to Europe. Then, after calling at the hotel to collect their luggage, they, too, went off to find the boat.

Three o'clock struck. The *Tankadere* was ready to raise its sails.

Besides John Bunsby there were four men on the boat – four strong and clever sailors who knew the China Sea perfectly. John Bunsby himself, a man of about forty-five years old, with sharp eyes and an active body, was a person whom anyone could trust.

Phileas and Aouda went on board. Fix was already there. They all went down into a small, but clean, cabin.

'I am sorry not to be able to offer you anything better than this,' said Mr Fogg to Fix.

The detective felt uncomfortable. He was not happy about being on the receiving end of Mr Fogg's kindness.

'He's a very polite thief,' Fix reminded himself, 'but he is a thief, all the same.'

At ten minutes past three the sails were raised. Mr Fogg and Aouda were standing on the ship's deck looking at the land for the last time in case Passepartout appeared.

Fix was clearly anxious. The unfortunate Frenchman, whom he had treated so badly, might still come, and then there would be an explanation not at all to the liking of the detective. But he did not appear. No doubt he was still suffering from what he had been given to drink.

Then John Bunsby threw off the ropes, and the *Tankadere* made its way at great speed towards the north.

Chapter 10   The Storm

A journey of 800 miles on a ship of this sort was not without danger. The China Seas are generally rough, particularly at this time of year. As the captain was being paid by the day, he would certainly have earned more money by going to Yokohama. But the journey to Shanghai was already dangerous enough.

During the last hours of the day, the *Tankadere* made its way through the narrow stretches of water to the north of Hong Kong.

'I hardly need tell you, Captain,' said Phileas Fogg, as the boat reached the open sea, 'how important it is to go as fast as possible.'

'Trust me,' answered John Bunsby. 'We are carrying as much sail as the wind will allow us.'

'It's your business, Captain, and not mine. I put my trust in you.'

Phileas Fogg, standing up straight like a sailor, fearlessly watched the rough waves. The young woman, seated near him, was looking, too, at the dark green water as it rushed by, thinking, no doubt, of her future. Above them floated the white sails, and the ship flew forward as a bird flies through the air.

Night came. The moon was in its first quarter, and clouds from the east had already covered a good part of the sky.

Fix was in the front part of the ship. He kept away from the others, knowing that Fogg disliked talking. Besides, he did not want to talk to the man from whom he had accepted so much kindness. He, too, was thinking of the future. He felt certain that

Fogg would not stop at Yokohama, but would immediately take the San Francisco boat for America, where he would be safe. Fogg's plan seemed to be a good one.

Instead of travelling directly from England to America, as most people in his position would have done, he preferred to sail round three-quarters of the earth to reach America more safely. There, having successfully escaped from the police, he would spend the money that he had stolen. But what would Fix do when they reached America? Would he give up the chase? No, a hundred times no! He would follow him until he caught him. It was his duty, and he would do his duty to the end. In any case, one fortunate thing had happened. Passepartout was no longer with his master, and after what Fix had said to him, it was important that master and servant should meet no more.

Phileas Fogg, too, was thinking about his servant, who had disappeared in such a strange way. Perhaps he had, after all, managed to sail on the *Carnatic*. Aouda also thought it possible. She was very sorry to lose the honest Frenchman to whom she owed her life. They might, though, find him at Yokohama, and it should not be difficult to discover whether the *Carnatic* had taken him there or not.

At about ten o'clock the wind grew stronger. At midnight Phileas Fogg and Aouda went down to the cabin. Fix was already there and asleep. The captain and his men stayed on deck all night.

By the next day, 8th November, the boat had gone more than a hundred miles. Its speed was between eight and nine miles an hour. There was plenty of wind in the sails, and at this rate the boat had every chance of achieving the distance in good time. The *Tankadere* kept close to the coast, and the sea was running in the right direction.

Mr Fogg and the young woman, neither of whom suffered from seasickness, enjoyed a good meal. Fix was asked to join them, and had to accept, but once again he was not happy about the situation. For Fogg to pay for his journey and his meals seemed too much – it was not really quite fair. All the same he had his meal.

But at the end of the meal he thought it his duty to take Mr Fogg to one side and, although he did not like addressing a thief as 'sir', he said: 'Sir, you have been kind enough to offer me transport on this boat. I am not rich enough to pay as much as I would like, but let me–'

'We will not speak of that, sir,' answered Mr Fogg.

'But, please–'

'No, sir,' said Fogg. 'I count it as part of the cost of my journey.'

Fix did not say another word for the rest of the day.

The ship sailed well. John Bunsby had high hopes. More than once he said to Mr Fogg that they would get to Shanghai in time. Mr Fogg simply answered that he depended on it. Thinking of the rich reward they would receive, the sailors worked hard, and by that evening they were 200 miles from Hong Kong.

Early in the morning the *Tankadere* was sailing between the island of Formosa and the coast of China. The sea was very rough and the movements of the ship were so violent that the travellers had some difficulty in standing up. When the sun rose, the wind blew more strongly and the sky was covered with black clouds.

The captain looked at the sky. He was feeling anxious.

'Do you mind if I tell you the truth?' he asked Fogg.

'Tell me everything,' answered Fogg.

'Well, we are going to have a storm.'

'Is it coming from the south or north?'

'From the south.'

'That is good news, then, since it will blow us in the right direction,' said Mr Fogg.

'If that is your opinion on the matter, I have nothing more to say,' answered the captain.

John Bunsby was right, and storms in the China Sea at this

time of the year are severe. All the sails except one were taken down. All the doors and other openings were tied shut so that no water could come in. They waited.

John Bunsby begged his passengers to go down below, but it would not have been pleasant to be shut up in the cabin, where there was little air. Mr Fogg and Aouda, and even Mr Fix, refused to leave the deck.

At about eight o'clock the storm broke. Rain poured down. Even with one sail the ship flew over the water. All that day waves poured over the sides. When evening came the wind changed direction and began to blow from the north-west. The waves struck the side of the ship and made it roll terribly. It was fortunate that the *Tankadere* was so solidly built.

As night came, the storm grew more violent. John Bunsby and his men were very worried. The captain went up to Mr Fogg and said: 'I think, sir, that we had better try to find a port.'

'I think so, too,' answered Phileas Fogg.

'But which one?'

'I only know of one.'

'And which is that?'

'Shanghai.'

It took the captain a few moments to understand what this answer meant. Then he said: 'Very well, sir, you are right. Let us go to Shanghai.'

And so the *Tankadere* kept on its way to the north, but more slowly. It was a terrible night. It was a wonder that the ship did not sink. More than once Mr Fogg had to rush to protect Aouda from the waves.

At last daylight came. The storm was still violent, but the wind changed to the south-east. This was better, and the ship flew forward again. Sometimes the coast of China could be seen, but there was not a ship in sight. The *Tankadere* was alone on the sea.

At midday the sea was a little calmer, and when the sun went down the wind blew less violently. The travellers were now able to take a little food and to rest.

The night was fairly calm, so the captain put up more sails and the ship moved at a good speed. The next morning, the morning of the 11th, John Bunsby was able to say that they were not more than a hundred miles from Shanghai.

A hundred miles, and there was only this one day in which to sail the distance. If they were to catch the steamer for Yokohama, they must reach Shanghai that same evening. Without the storm, during which they had lost several hours, they would now have been only thirty miles away.

The wind blew much less strongly, and the sea grew calmer at the same time. All the sails were put up. At midday the *Tankadere* was not more than forty-five miles from Shanghai, but only six hours were left in which to catch the boat. All those on the ship feared that the time was too short. It was necessary to sail at the speed of nine miles an hour, but the wind was weakening all the time. The ship was light and fast though, and the sails picked up the little wind there was. So at six o'clock John Bunsby found himself about ten miles from the mouth of the Shanghai River – the town itself is twelve miles further up the river.

At seven o'clock they were three miles away. The captain swore – he was certainly going to lose his reward of two hundred pounds. He looked at Mr Fogg. Mr Fogg was perfectly calm, in spite of the fact that his whole fortune was in danger.

At that moment a long black chimney came into sight, with black smoke pouring out of it. It was the American steamer sailing from Shanghai at its usual time.

'Signal to them,' said Phileas Fogg.

A small cannon on deck was used to send signals during bad weather. John Bunsby filled it with gunpowder.

'Fire!' said Mr Fogg.

And the cannon roared.

Chapter 11   Passepartout Has No Money

The *Carnatic* left Hong Kong on 7th November, at half past six in the evening, and sailed at full steam towards Japan. It carried many passengers, but there were three empty cabins – those that should have been used by Mr Fogg.

The next morning the men on deck saw, with some surprise, a passenger with an unwashed face and hair in complete disorder come out from a second-class cabin onto the deck, and fall into a chair. It was Passepartout. This is what had happened.

A few moments after Fix had left the bar, two Chinese men saw Passepartout sleeping on the floor. They lifted him up and laid him on the bed among the other sleepers. But three hours later, remembering even in his dreams that there was a duty that he had left undone, the poor man woke up and fought against his sleepiness and the poison of the drink in his blood. He got up with difficulty and, holding himself up by keeping close to the walls, managed to find his way into the street.

'The *Carnatic*, the *Carnatic*,' he cried, as if in a dream.

Somehow he made his way to the port. The steamer was there and preparing to leave. Passepartout climbed on board and, at exactly the moment when the ship started, fell senseless onto the deck.

Some of the sailors, used to seeing this sort of thing, carried him down to a cabin, and Passepartout slept until the following morning, when they were a 150 miles from Hong Kong.

That is how it was, then, that he found himself on the deck of the *Carnatic*. The fresh air brought him to his senses. He began to remember, but with some difficulty, what had happened to him: the drinking hall, what Fix had told him, and all the rest.

'I must have been terribly drunk,' he thought. 'What will Mr Fogg say to me? Well, I have caught the boat, and that is the main thing.'

Then he thought about Fix.

'We shall see no more of him, I hope. After what he said to me he will not dare follow us on the *Carnatic*. A detective, he calls himself, a detective wanting to arrest my master for stealing money from the Bank of England!'

Passepartout began wondering whether he should tell the story to his master. Ought he to let him know about Fix? Would it not be better to wait until they got to London, and then to tell him how a detective had followed him round the world? What a joke that would be! Yes, that would be the best thing to do. Anyhow, it was worth considering. The most important thing now was to go and join his master and beg forgiveness for his behaviour of the night before.

So Passepartout got up from his chair. The sea was rather rough and the boat was rolling heavily. He walked as well as he could, up and down the deck, but saw nobody at all who was like Mr Fogg or Aouda.

'Very well,' he thought. 'The lady has probably not got up yet, and Mr Fogg has found somebody to play cards with.'

So he went down below deck. Mr Fogg was not there. He then went to the office to ask which was Mr Fogg's cabin. The man at the office said that there was nobody of that name on the boat.

'But excuse me,' said Passepartout. 'He must be on the boat.' He then gave the officer a description of Mr Fogg, saying that there was a young lady with him.

'We have no young ladies on board,' answered the officer. 'Here is a list of passengers; you can see for yourself.'

Passepartout looked at the list. His master's name was not there. A sudden idea struck him.

'Am I on the *Carnatic*?'

'Yes,' answered the officer.

'On the way to Yokohama?'

'Certainly.'

Passepartout had been afraid for a moment that he was on the wrong boat. But if it was true that he was on the *Carnatic*, it was certain that his master was not.

Then he remembered everything. He remembered how the hour of sailing had been changed, that he was going to warn his master and that he had not done so. It was his fault, then, that Mr Fogg and his companion had not caught the boat!

His fault, yes. But it was still more the fault of the man who had taken him to a bar and had made him drunk in order to keep his master in Hong Kong. And now Mr Fogg had certainly lost his bet; he had, perhaps been arrested; he might even be in prison! At this thought the Frenchman tore his hair. Ah! If he ever got hold of Fix, how he would pay him back for what he had done!

When the first terrible moments of his discovery had passed, Passepartout grew calmer and began to examine his position. It was not a happy one. He was on his way to Japan. He was certain to get there, but how would he get away again? His pockets were empty; he had no money at all. But his cabin and food had been paid for, so he had five or six days in front of him during which time he could make some plans for the future.

It is impossible to describe how much he ate and drank during this part of the journey. He ate and drank for his master, for Aouda and for himself. He ate as if Japan were a country in which there was no food at all.

◆

On the morning of the 13th, the *Carnatic* reached Yokohama and tied up among a large number of ships that had come from nearly all the countries of the world.

Passepartout, feeling rather frightened, got off the boat in this strange Land of the Rising Sun. All that he could do was to be guided by chance and go walking about the streets. He first found himself in the European part of the town where, as in Hong

Kong, the streets were crowded with people of every nationality – traders who seemed ready to buy or to sell anything. Among all these people Passepartout felt as lonely as if he had been thrown into the middle of Africa.

There was certainly one thing that he could do – he could go to the French and British consuls. He very much disliked, though, the idea of telling his story and the story of his master to these government officials. He would go to the consuls only if everything else failed.

He then went to the Japanese part of the town, where he saw the temples and strangely designed houses. The streets here, too, were crowded with people: priests; officers dressed in silk and carrying two swords; soldiers with their blue and white coats, carrying guns; fishermen; beggars, and large numbers of children.

Passepartout walked around among these people for some hours, looking at the strange sights, the shops, the eating houses and the amusement halls. But in the shops he could see neither meat nor bread; and even if he had seen any, he had no money.

The next morning he felt very tired and hungry. He would certainly have to eat something, and the sooner the better. He could, of course, have sold his watch, but he would rather die of hunger than do that. Now was the time when he could use the strong, if not very musical, voice that nature had given him. He knew a few French and English songs, and he made up his mind to try them.

But perhaps it was rather early in the day to start singing. It might be better to wait a few hours. The thought then came to him that he was too well dressed for a street singer. He would do well to change his clothes for others more suitable to his position. Besides, by doing so he might make a little money with which to buy food.

It was some time before he found a shop where they bought and sold old clothes. The owner of the shop liked the look of what Passepartout was wearing, and soon Passepartout came out dressed in Japanese clothes – old ones, it is true, but quite comfortable. What pleased him most were the few pieces of silver that he had been given as part of the arrangement.

The next thing that Passepartout did was to go to a small eating house, where he was able to satisfy his hunger.

'Now,' he thought, 'I have no time to lose. I had better make my stay in this Land of the Rising Sun as short as possible.'

His idea was to visit any steamers going to America. He could offer his services as cook or servant, asking for nothing except his food and transport. If he could get to San Francisco, he would be all right. The important thing was to cross the 4,700 miles of sea between Japan and the New World. So he headed for the port.

But as he got near, his plan, which had seemed so simple when he made it, now seemed to be more and more impossible to carry out. Why would they need a cook or a servant on an American boat, and what would any captain or officer think of him, dressed as he was? Then again he had no papers to show, no letters from people expressing their satisfaction at his service.

While he was thinking matters over, he saw in front of an amusement hall a large noticeboard:

William Batulcar's
Company of Japanese Acrobats

Last Performances
before leaving for America
of the
Long Noses!
Come and see them!

'America!' cried Passepartout. 'Just what I wanted.'
He went inside the building and asked for Mr Batulcar. A few

minutes later Mr Batulcar appeared.

'What do you want?' he asked, mistaking Passepartout for a poor Japanese man.

'Do you want a servant?' asked Passepartout.

'A servant,' cried the man. 'I have two strong and honest servants who have always been with me, who serve me for nothing except food. And here they are!' he added, showing two strong arms.

'So I can be of no help to you?'

'None.'

'That's a pity. It would have suited me to go with you to America.'

'Oh,' answered Mr Batulcar, 'you are no more Japanese than I am. Why are you dressed like that?'

'A man dresses as he can!'

'That's true. You are a Frenchman?'

'Yes.'

'Then I suppose you can make funny faces.'

'Well,' answered Passepartout, who did not like this question at all, 'we Frenchmen can certainly make funny faces, but they are no funnier than American faces!'

'Quite right. Are you strong?'

'Yes.'

'Can you sing?'

'Yes.'

'Can you sing while you are standing on your hands?'

'Oh, yes,' answered Passepartout, thinking of the acrobatic tricks he had done when he was young.

'Very well, then, I will take you.'

So Passepartout had found a position with this company of Japanese acrobats. It was not a very pleasant way of earning his living, but in a week's time he would be on his way to San Francisco.

At three o'clock that afternoon the hall was filled with people who had come to see the acrobats do their tricks. One of the most amusing acts was that of the company of the Long Noses. Each of the acrobats had a piece of wood stuck on the front of his face which gave the appearance of an extremely long nose. One of the things they had to do as a group was to form a pyramid with their bodies. But instead of climbing on each other's shoulders, as is usual, the artists were to stand on top of the noses. One of the most important positions was in the middle of the bottom row, since this particular nose supported most of the weight of the people above him. The man who had always been in this position had suddenly left the company, so Passepartout had been chosen to take his place.

He felt rather sad when he put on the fine clothes that he was to wear – it made him think of his younger days – and when the long nose was fitted to his face. But, as this nose was going to earn him something to eat, he felt happier.

Passepartout came in with the first group of acrobats and they all stretched themselves out on the ground with their noses pointing to the ceiling. A second group came and stood on the noses. A third group took their positions on the noses of the others, then came a fourth, until the pyramid reached the top of the hall. The music began to play and great was the admiration of all who were watching. Suddenly, though, the pyramid began to shake. One of the lower noses disappeared from his key position, and the whole pyramid fell.

It was Passepartout's fault. He jumped down from the stage and fell at the feet of a gentleman who was watching, crying: 'Ah! My master! My master!'

'You?'

'Yes, I.'

'Well, in that case, let us go to the steamer.'

Mr Fogg, Aouda, who was with him, and Passepartout quickly

went outside, where they found Mr Batulcar shouting angrily. He wanted to be paid for the breaking of the pyramid. Phileas Fogg calmed him by giving him a number of bank notes. And at half past six, just as it was about to leave, Mr Fogg and Aouda went on board the American steamer, followed by Passepartout, who still had his six-foot-long nose stuck onto his face!

◆

It is clear now what had happened at Shanghai. The signals made by the *Tankadere* had been noticed by the Yokohama steamer. The captain of the steamer, hearing the noise of the cannon and thinking that help was needed, went towards the smaller boat. A few moments later, Phileas Fogg paid John Bunsby the money that had been promised. Then Mr Fogg and Aouda and Fix climbed on the steamer, which made its way first to Nagasaki and then to Yokohama.

Having arrived there that very morning, 14th November, Phileas Fogg immediately went on board the *Carnatic*. There he received the information, to the great joy of Aouda − perhaps even of himself, though he gave no sign of it − that Passepartout had come by that boat and had reached Yokohama the night before.

Phileas Fogg, who was planning to leave that evening for San Francisco, began to look for his servant. He visited, but without success, the French and British consuls. He walked around the streets of Yokohama and, having almost lost hope of finding Passepartout, wandered almost by chance into Mr Batulcar's hall. Passepartout, even in his position on the floor, saw him immediately, and in his excitement could not keep his nose from moving. The result of this movement was the fall of the pyramid.

All this Passepartout heard from Aouda, who told him of their journey from Hong Kong to Yokohama in the company of a Mr Fix. When he heard the name of Fix, Passepartout made no sign.

He thought that the moment had not yet come to tell his master what had passed between the detective and himself. So, when giving an account of his own adventures, he simply expressed his sadness at having had too much drink in a bar in Hong Kong.

Mr Fogg listened to the story coldly and did not answer, but he gave his servant enough money to get some new clothes. Passepartout was able to buy clothes on the ship, and an hour later he looked very different from the long-nosed acrobat of Yokohama.

Chapter 12   Crossing the Pacific Ocean

The boat carrying them from Yokohama to San Francisco was the *General Grant*, which belonged to the American Steamship Company. It was a large steamer, well built and able to travel at great speed. At the rate of twelve miles an hour it would take only twenty-one days to cross the Pacific Ocean. Phileas Fogg had every reason to believe that he would be in San Francisco on 2nd December, in New York on the 11th, and that he would reach London on the 20th, a few hours earlier than the 21st.

There were a good number of people on the boat: English, Americans, and others.

During the crossing nothing in particular happened. The sea was calm. Mr Fogg was calm, too, and said little, as usual. Aouda came to have more and more respect for this man who had done so much for her. In fact, almost unconsciously, her feelings of respect were changing to feelings of a different sort.

Whatever her feelings may have been, she was very interested in this gentleman's plan, and most anxious that nothing might happen to spoil it. She often had talks with Passepartout, who soon saw the state of her feelings towards Mr Fogg. He praised his master's honesty and kindness. Then he calmed her anxieties about the journey, saying that the most difficult part was already over. They had left those strange countries of China and Japan; and if they crossed America by train and the Atlantic Ocean by steamer, it would be easy to complete the journey round the world in good time.

Nine days after leaving Yokohama, Phileas Fogg had gone round exactly one half of the world. It is true that out of the eighty days he had used up fifty-two. But we must remember that if Mr Fogg had done half the journey as measured by the sun, he had really done more than two-thirds in distance as measured by the number of miles travelled. From London to Aden, Aden to Bombay, Calcutta to Singapore, Singapore to Yokohama – that was a very indirect journey. If we could go round the world as the sun does, the distance from London to London would be 12,000 miles. But by this indirect journey the distance is 26,000 miles, of which Mr Fogg had travelled 17,500. From now on the journey would be almost in a straight line. And Fix was no longer there to stop him.

It happened, too, that on this day, 23th November, Passepartout made a discovery that brought him great joy. It will be remembered that his watch kept London time, and that he refused to put its hands forward. All the clocks in all the countries he had passed through, he said, were wrong. Now on this day, although he had put its hands neither forward nor backward, the watch showed the same time as the clock on the ship. He wished that Fix were there so that he could prove to him that his watch kept the right time after all.

'The silly fool was talking to me about the sun and the moon and the movement of the earth. If we listened to people like him, we would have a very funny sort of time. I was certain that one day the sun would come to agree with my watch!'

But there was something that Passepartout did not know. If his watch had been marked from one to twenty-four hours (as some clocks are) he would not have been so happy about it. For in that case, instead of pointing to nine o'clock (as it did), it would have been pointing to twenty-one hours.

But if Fix had been able to explain this, Passepartout would not have been able to understand the explanation, or to accept it. In any case, if the detective had appeared at that moment, it is probable that Passepartout would have had something to say to him on quite a different subject.

But where *was* Fix at that moment?

He was, in fact, on the *General Grant*.

When he reached Yokohama, he left Mr Fogg, whom he expected to meet again later in the day, and went immediately to the British consul. There he found the warrant. It had been following him all the way from Bombay, and was already forty days old. It had been sent on from Hong Kong by the *Carnatic*, the steamer on which he was believed to be. We may imagine the disappointment of Fix – the warrant had now become useless because Mr Fogg was outside the reach of the English law.

'Very well!' Fix said to himself, swallowing his anger. 'The warrant is of no use here, but it will be of use in England. It looks as if this bank robber intends to return home after all. Very well, I will follow him there. As for the money he stole, I hope there will still be some left. But with the cost of the journey, the presents he gives, the elephant he bought, and the rest, my man must have left more than five thousand pounds behind along the way. It is a good thing that the Bank of England is so rich.'

Having made up his mind, he went to the *General Grant*, and was there when Mr Fogg and Aouda came on board. To his great surprise he also saw Passepartout in his strange clothes and long nose, so he hid in his cabin. There were so many passengers that he hoped his enemy would not see him. But today, towards the front of the ship, he suddenly met him.

Without saying a word, Passepartout jumped on Fix and, to

the great joy of a group of Americans (who immediately began to bet on the result of the fight), attacked him, striking him again and again.

When he had hit him a number of times, Passepartout felt much better and calmer. Fix got up slowly.

'Have you finished?' he asked coldly.

'Yes, for the moment.'

'Then come and have a talk with me.'

'Have a talk with you! I—'

'Yes, if you care about your master.'

Passepartout was so surprised by the calm way in which Fix spoke that he followed him. They both sat down.

'You have given me a beating. Very well, I expected it. Now listen to me. Until now I have been your master's enemy, but now I am on his side.'

'Oh, at last, then, you believe him to be an honest man.'

'No, I don't,' answered Fix coldly, 'I believe him to be a thief. Be quiet, and let me speak. So long as Fogg was on British soil I tried to hold him back while I was waiting for the warrant to arrest him. I did all that I could do to stop him. I sent the priests from Bombay to Calcutta; I made you drunk at Hong Kong; I separated you from him and made him miss the boat to Yokohama.'

Passepartout listened, ready to fly at Fix again.

'Now,' Fix went on, 'Mr Fogg seems to be going back to England. Very well, I will follow him. But from now on, I will help him in his journey as much as I have tried to stop his journey in the past. You see that my plan has changed. It has changed because it is in my interest to change it. I will add that your interest is the same as mine, since it is only in England that you will know whether you are serving an honest man or a thief.'

Passepartout listened carefully to what Fix was saying, and felt sure that Fix was not going to play any more tricks.

'Are we friends?' asked Fix.

'No, not friends,' answered Passepartout, 'but we can help each other. If you start playing any more games with me, though, I will certainly break your neck!'

'All right,' agreed the detective calmly.

Chapter 13 A Quarrel in San Francisco

Eleven days later, on 3rd December, the *General Grant* reached San Francisco. Mr Fogg was neither a day too late nor a day too early.

As soon as he got on shore he asked what time the first train left for New York. The answer was: 'At six o'clock this evening.' Mr Fogg had, then, a whole day to spend in San Francisco. He called a carriage and he and his friends drove to the International Hotel.

After a good meal, Mr Fogg went with Aouda to the British consul to show his passport and have it signed.

When they came out, Mr Fogg found his servant waiting.

'As we are going to travel through a wild part of the country where we might be attacked by Indians or train robbers, would it not be wise to buy a few revolvers with which to protect ourselves?' asked Passepartout.

Mr Fogg answered that he thought that was not at all necessary, but Passepartout could go and buy some if he liked.

Phileas Fogg had hardly walked a hundred steps when he met Fix. The detective seemed to be most surprised at this meeting.

'What a strange thing!' he said, 'that we should meet by chance like this. To think that we both travelled on the *General Grant* without once seeing each other.'

Fix was most pleased, he said, to meet again the gentleman to whom he owed so much. He was forced to go back to Europe on business, and it would be very pleasant if they could travel together.

Mr Fogg answered that the honour would be his. Fix, who did not wish to lose sight of the man he was following, asked to be allowed to join him in a walk around the city.

So Aouda, Phileas Fogg and Fix walked through the streets. Before long they saw crowds of excited people. Some were shouting, 'Long live Kamerfield!' and others, 'Mandiboy for ever!'

'This seems to be an election,' said Fix to Mr Fogg. 'Perhaps it would be a good idea to keep away from the crowd, or we might get hurt.' Fix was now very anxious that nothing should happen to Mr Fogg. It was in his interest to take care of him and protect him from harm, so that he could arrest him when they reached England.

'You are right,' answered Phileas Fogg and he, Aouda and Fix went and stood at the top of some stone steps where they could see what was going on below.

At that moment the crowd became very excited. People rushed here and there, shouting loudly. Fix was just going to ask somebody what all this meant, when a general fight broke out. Stones and bottles were thrown, and sticks were used freely. A group of people moved onto the steps below, shouting loudly.

'I think we had better leave,' said Fix.

'They cannot hurt us; we are English—' Mr Fogg began to say, but before he could finish, another noisy group came up behind them. They were caught between the two groups, which became increasingly violent. No escape was possible. Phileas Fogg and Fix, in protecting the young lady, were knocked this way and that. Mr Fogg, as calm as ever, tried to defend himself, but a big man with red hair raised his hand over Mr Fogg to strike a violent blow. Mr Fogg would have suffered serious damage if Fix had not received the blow in Mr Fogg's place.

'Fool of an American!' said Mr Fogg, looking at his attacker.

'Fool of an Englishman!' answered the other.

'We shall meet again!'

'When you like. Your name?'

'Phileas Fogg. Your name?'

'Stamp W. Proctor.'

At that moment the crowd moved on. Fix stood up slowly; his clothes were torn, but he was not seriously hurt.

'Thank you,' said Mr Fogg to the detective, as soon as they were out of the crowd.

'Do not thank me,' answered Fix, 'but come with me.'

'Where?'

'To a shop where we can buy some new clothes.'

It was in fact quite necessary to do this; as a result of the fight, the clothes of both men had been torn to pieces. An hour later, wearing new hats and coats, they returned to the hotel.

Passepartout was waiting for his master. He was holding the revolvers that he had been buying. He looked anxious when he saw Fix with his master, but when Aouda explained to him what had happened, he became more cheerful. It was clear that Fix was keeping his promise and was no longer an enemy.

When dinner was over, Mr Fogg sent for a carriage to take the travellers and their luggage to the station. Mr Fogg said to Fix: 'Do you know anything about this Stamp W. Proctor?'

'No,' answered Fix.

'I shall come back from England to find him again,' said Phileas Fogg. 'It is not right that an Englishman should be treated as he treated me.'

At a quarter to six the travellers reached the station and found the train ready to start.

The railway on which they were travelling runs from San Francisco to New York, a distance of 3,786 miles. As the journey took seven days, Mr Fogg would reach New York just in time to take the steamer that left for Liverpool on 11th December.

The travellers left Oakland Station at six o'clock. It was already dark, and the sky was covered with black clouds. The train did not move with any great speed; perhaps twenty miles an hour, with many stops.

Nobody talked much. Passepartout found himself sitting next to the detective, but he did not speak to him. There was a certain coldness between the two – and this was only natural.

An hour later it began to snow.

At eight o'clock the travellers were told that it was time to get the beds ready for the night, and in a few minutes their carriage looked more like a bedroom. There was only one thing to do, and that was to sleep. And while the travellers were sleeping, the train steamed across California.

It took six hours for the train to reach the city of Sacramento. From San Francisco the country had been fairly flat, but now the train began to climb into the mountains of Nevada. At seven o'clock the train passed through Cisco.

An hour later the beds were packed away, and the travellers looked out of the windows and were able to see the mountainous country through which they were passing. There were few or no bridges. The train ran up and round the sides of the mountains or passed along the bottom of the narrow valleys.

At Reno the travellers stopped for twenty minutes, during which time they were able to have breakfast. Then they took their places again in their carriages and looked at the scenery through which they were passing. At times they saw large numbers of buffaloes. By crossing the railway line in their thousands, these animals often force the trains to stop and wait until they have passed and this, in fact, is what soon happened. At about twelve o'clock the train came to a place where ten or twelve thousand buffaloes were walking slowly across the line. It was impossible to move them or go through this solid body of animals. The only thing to do was to wait until the line was clear.

The travellers watched this strange sight with interest. Phileas Fogg stayed in his seat and waited patiently. But Passepartout was terribly angry, and very much wanted to start shooting them with his revolvers.

'What a terrible country!' he cried. 'A country where animals like these are allowed to get in the way of trains! I wonder whether Mr Fogg expected this sort of thing when he planned his journey. And here is the engine driver afraid of running his engine through them.'

The engine driver, of course, was wise enough not even to consider such an action. It would have been useless. He could no doubt have crushed the first buffaloes, but the engine would soon have been stopped and probably thrown off the line.

It was three hours before the last of the animals crossed the railway, and it was dark before the train could go on again.

By 7th December they had gone a long way. On this day they stopped for a quarter of an hour at Green River Station. It had been snowing and raining during the night, but as the snow had half melted it gave no trouble. The bad weather worried Passepartout, though.

'What a foolish idea it was to go travelling during the winter,' he said to himself. 'If my master had waited for better weather, he would have had a better chance of winning his bet.'

But while Passepartout was worrying about the weather, Aouda began to be frightened about something much more serious. Looking out of the window, she saw among the group of travellers Stamp W. Proctor, the man who had behaved so roughly in the election fight at San Francisco. It was only by accident that he was travelling on the same train, but there he was. 'He must be prevented,' she thought, 'from meeting Mr Fogg.'

When the train was on its way again, and Mr Fogg had fallen asleep, Aouda told Fix and Passepartout whom she had seen.

'Proctor on this train!' cried Fix. 'Have no fear; it is my business rather than Mr Fogg's. After all, I am the one who suffered most.'

'And I shall have something to say to him, too,' added Passepartout.

'Mr Fix,' said Aouda, 'you may be certain that Mr Fogg will let nobody take his place in this matter. He said he would even come back to America to meet this man again. If he sees Mr Proctor, we cannot prevent them from fighting, and this might not end well. They must not meet each other.'

'You are right,' said Fix. 'A fight might ruin everything. Whether he won or lost, Mr Fogg would be delayed, and–'

'And that would suit the gentlemen of the Reform Club,' added Passepartout. 'In four days we shall be in New York! Well, if during those four days Mr Fogg does not leave his carriage, we may hope that he will not meet this man.'

At this moment Mr Fogg woke up, and the discussion came to an end. Later, without being heard by his master or Aouda, Passepartout said to the detective: 'Would you really fight instead of him?'

'I will do everything to bring him back alive to Europe,' answered Fix.

Was there any way to keep Mr Fogg in the carriage to prevent him from meeting this Proctor? It should not be difficult, for Mr Fogg did not enjoy moving around. In any case, the detective had a good plan and, a few minutes later, said to him: 'Time passes very slowly in the train.'

'Yes,' answered the other, 'but it passes all the same.'

'On the boat,' said Fix, 'you used to play cards.'

'Yes,' answered Phileas Fogg, 'but here it would be difficult. I have neither cards nor people to play with.'

'Oh we can easily buy the cards; they are sold on all American trains. As for people to play with, if by chance the lady plays . . .'

'Oh, yes,' answered the lady. 'I know the game that Mr Fogg likes playing.'

'So do I,' said Fix. 'In fact I am quite good at cards. So perhaps the three of us . . .'

'Very well; if you would like to,' answered Phileas Fogg, who was very pleased to have the chance of playing again.

Passepartout was sent to get the cards, and soon came back with everything that was necessary for the game. A table was brought and a cloth was laid over it, and they started playing. Aouda really played very well, and Mr Fogg told her so. As for Fix, he was a first-class player.

'Now,' thought Passepartout, 'everything is going to be fine. He will not move from the table.'

Chapter 14 Full Speed!

At eleven o'clock in the morning the train had climbed to one of the highest points on its journey through the Rocky Mountains. Two hundred miles further on they would reach those wide stretches of flat country that lie between the mountains and the Atlantic coast. So in a few hours they would have passed the difficult and dangerous part of their journey through the mountains.

After a good meal the travellers began playing cards again. But before long the train moved more and more slowly and then came to a complete stop. Passepartout put his head out of the window and could see nothing that might explain the delay. There was no station in the area.

For a moment Aouda and Fix were afraid that Mr Fogg would want to get off the train. But he only turned to Passepartout and said: 'Go and see what's the matter.'

Passepartout jumped out. Thirty or forty travellers had got off, and among them was Stamp W. Proctor.

The train had stopped in front of a red signal. The engine

driver and the guard were talking very seriously to a man who had been sent from the next station to stop the train. Some of the travellers came up and joined in the discussion – among them Mr Stamp W. Proctor, with his rough, loud voice.

Passepartout heard the man say: 'No, you can't possibly get past! The bridge at Medicine Bow is in need of repair, and will certainly not support the weight of the train.'

The bridge of which they were talking was one that hung across a deep river about a mile further on. What the man said was clearly quite true; the bridge was unsafe.

Passepartout, not daring to go and inform his master, stayed and listened.

'Well,' said Mr Proctor, 'we are not going to stand here for ever in the snow!'

'Sir,' answered the guard, 'we have sent a telegram to Omaha asking them to send a train to meet us at Medicine Bow, but it can hardly get here in less than six hours.'

'Six hours!' cried Passepartout.

'Yes,' said the guard. 'In any case it will take us that time to walk as far as the station.'

'Walk?' cried all the travellers.

'How far away is the station, then?' asked someone.

'It is only a mile away, but it is on the other side of the river. We shall have to walk to reach a safe crossing. It will be a distance of fifteen miles in all.'

'A fifteen-mile walk in the snow!' cried Stamp W. Proctor. Then he started shouting, swearing, calling the railway company and its officials all the bad names he could think of. Passepartout, who was equally angry, felt like joining him. But here was something that it was no use fighting about. All his master's bank notes were useless in the face of this difficulty.

The passengers were extremely disappointed and upset. Not only would they be late, but they would also have to walk fifteen miles through the snow. The noise of their complaints would certainly have been noticed by Phileas Fogg if that gentleman had not been so interested in his game.

Passepartout saw that he would have to tell his master what had happened. He was just walking towards the carriage, when the engine driver, a true American by the name of Foster, raised his voice and said: 'Gentlemen, there is one way of getting across.'

'Across the bridge?' asked somebody.

'Yes, across the bridge.'

'With our train?' asked Proctor.

'With our train.'

Passepartout stopped, and listened to what was being said.

'But the bridge is unsafe!'

'That doesn't matter,' said the engine driver. 'I believe that by sending the train across at full speed, there will be a good chance of getting over.'

'Well, what a crazy idea!' thought Passepartout.

But quite a number of the travellers very much liked the idea, particularly Stamp W. Proctor.

'Quite reasonable and quite natural!' he cried. 'Why,' he went on, 'there are engineers who are now designing trains that, travelling at full speed, can cross rivers without any bridge at all!'

In the end all the travellers agreed to the idea. Passepartout was too surprised to speak. He was ready to attempt anything in order to get across the river, but this seemed to him to be rather too 'American'.

'Besides,' he thought, 'there is a much simpler way, and these people have not even thought of it.'

'Sir,' he said to one of the travellers, 'the plan seems to me a little dangerous, but–'

'There is nothing more to be said,' answered the man. 'The engine driver says we can get across, and that is an end of the matter.'

'Yes, I am sure we can get across,' said Passepartout, 'but would it not be less dangerous—'

'What's that! Dangerous?' cried Proctor. 'Don't you understand? At full speed!'

'Yes, I understand,' said Passepartout, trying again to finish what he wanted to say. 'But don't you think it would be a better idea—'

'What? What's that? What's he talking about?' everybody shouted.

'Are you afraid?' asked Proctor.

'Afraid? I, afraid?' cried Passepartout. 'I'll show these Americans whether a Frenchman is afraid!'

'Take your seats! Take your seats!' shouted the guard.

'All right! All right!' shouted Passepartout to him. 'But I can't help thinking that it would be safer for us to walk over the bridge first, and then to let the train follow!'

But nobody heard this wise advice, and in any case nobody would have agreed to the idea.

The travellers all went back to their seats, and Passepartout went back to his, without saying anything of what had happened. The card players were sitting there thinking only of their game.

The engine driver took the train back nearly a mile, in the same way as a jumper steps back before he makes his jump. Then he made it go forward again, more and more quickly, until the train was moving at a frightening speed. It seemed to be going at about 100 miles an hour. It flew over the bridge! Nobody even saw the bridge – the train simply jumped from one side of the river to the other, and the driver could not stop it until it was five miles the other side of the station.

But the train had hardly crossed over the river when the bridge fell with a crash into the water below.

◆

That evening the train reached the highest point of its journey. It now had only to go down until it reached the Atlantic. The travellers had come 1,382 miles from San Francisco in three days and three nights. In another four days and four nights they should be at New York.

The next day the three companions were playing cards as usual. None of them complained about the length of the journey. Fix had begun by winning a few pounds, and was now losing them again. Mr Fogg held very good cards, and he was just going to play one of them when a voice was heard behind him saying:

'Don't play that; play a diamond instead.'

Mr Fogg, Aouda and Fix looked up to see Stamp W. Proctor standing there.

'Oh, it's you, is it, Mr Englishman!' cried he. 'You are the one who wants to play a heart.'

'Yes, and I shall play it,' answered Phileas Fogg, as he did so.

'Well, I want you to play the diamond.' And the man bent forward to take hold of it, adding, 'You don't know how to play this game.'

'Perhaps there is another game that I know better,' said Phileas Fogg, getting up from his seat.

'Well, you can try,' replied Proctor with an ugly smile on his face.

Aouda looked very frightened. She took hold of Mr Fogg's arm, but he gently pushed her away. Passepartout was ready to throw himself on the American, but Fix stood up, went to Proctor, and said: 'The quarrel is between you and me. You were not only disrespectful towards me, but you even struck me.'

'Mr Fix,' said Mr Fogg, 'I beg your pardon, but this is my business alone. This man will answer to me for his behaviour.'

'When and where you like,' replied the American.

Aouda tried to hold Mr Fogg back, but without success. The detective attempted to take the quarrel on himself. Passepartout wanted to throw the American out of the window, but a sign from his master stopped him. Phileas Fogg left the carriage, and the American followed him.

'Sir,' said Mr Fogg to his enemy, 'after our meeting in San Francisco I made up my mind to come back to America to find you as soon as I had finished the business that calls me to England.'

'Really!'

'Will you meet me in six months' time?'

'Why not in six years' time?'

'I said six months,' answered Mr Fogg.

'You want to escape from me!' cried Stamp W. Proctor. 'You will fight me now or never.'

'Very well,' answered Mr Fogg. 'You are going to New York?'

'No.'

'Chicago?'

'No.'

'Omaha?'

'That's no business of yours. Do you know Plum Creek?'

'No,' answered Mr Fogg.

'It's the next station. The train will be there in an hour's time. It will wait there for ten minutes. That will give us time enough to fight.'

'Agreed,' said Mr Fogg. 'I will stop at Plum Creek.'

'And you will stay there!' said the American, with an ugly laugh.

'Who knows, sir?' answered Mr Fogg, returning to his seat. 'People who talk loudly are not to be feared,' he remarked to the anxious Aouda, to calm her. Then he took Fix on one side and asked him to help him prepare for the fight when the time came. Fix could not refuse, and Phileas Fogg picked up his cards and went on with his game.

At eleven o'clock the train reached Plum Creek Station and

stopped. Mr Fogg got up and, followed by Fix, left the carriage. Passepartout went too, carrying a pair of revolvers.

They had not been outside long when the door opened and Mr Proctor came out with a friend. But just as the two enemies were preparing themselves, the guard ran up, saying: 'Nobody is to get out here, gentlemen.'

'Why not?' asked Proctor, angrily.

'We are twenty minutes late, and the train is not going to wait.'

'But I have to fight this gentleman.'

'I am sorry,' said the guard, 'but we are starting immediately. There is the bell ringing.'

As he said this, the train started to move and the two men jumped on.

'I am really very sorry, gentlemen,' said the guard. 'I would like to have helped you. But as you have had no time to fight at Plum Creek, is there any reason why you should not fight on the train?'

'Perhaps that would not suit this gentleman,' said Proctor with an unpleasant laugh.

'It will suit me perfectly,' answered Phileas Fogg.

'We are certainly in America!' thought Passepartout. 'And the guard is a perfect gentleman!' He followed his master.

The two men, their friends and the guard passed through the carriages until they reached the end of the train. In the last carriage there were only about ten people. The official asked these passengers whether they would be good enough to give up the carriage for a few minutes to two gentlemen who wished to fight.

Well, of course! They were only too happy to be of any service to the two gentlemen, and immediately went out and stood in the passage.

The carriage was fifty feet long, and very suitable for the purpose. The two men could walk towards each other between the seats and shoot at each other without difficulty. Mr Fogg and

Mr Proctor, each carrying two revolvers, would go inside. The two supporters would shut the door and stay outside. A signal would be given, and shooting would begin. Then, after two minutes, the door would be opened and what was left of the two gentlemen would be carried out. Nothing could be simpler.

Chapter 15   An Attack by Indians

But before the signal could be given, wild cries and shots were heard. The shots certainly did not come from the carriage in which the two gentlemen had just been shut. Bang! Bang! Bang! The shots came from the outside – all along the train. Cries of terror were heard from one end of the train to the other.

Mr Proctor and Mr Fogg, with their revolvers in their hands, rushed out towards the front of the train, where shouts and shots were growing louder at every moment. They were under attack by Sioux Indians.

This was not the first time that these Indians had attacked a train, and more than once before they had been successful. In their usual way, a hundred of them had jumped on the steps of the moving train and had climbed up onto the roof of the carriages.

From these positions on and around the train, they fired their guns. The passengers answered with their revolvers. Some of the Indians had jumped on the engine and had injured the engine driver. One of them tried to stop the train but, not knowing how to do so, had opened the steam pipe instead of shutting it. The result was that the train was flying along at full speed.

Soon the Sioux forced their way into the carriages and were fighting with the passengers. The cries and shots continued without stopping.

But the passengers defended themselves bravely. Among these

was Aouda. With a revolver in her hand, she fired through the broken windows at any Indian that came in sight. Twenty or more of the Indians fell dead or wounded on the railway line, and the wheels crushed any who fell between the carriages. Several of the passengers were also badly wounded, and were lying on the seats.

The end must come before long. Fighting had been going on for ten minutes, and the Sioux would win unless the train were able to stop. Fort Kearney Station was only two miles away, and there were soldiers there; but if the train passed this point, the Sioux would certainly become masters of the train.

The guard was fighting at Mr Fogg's side when a shot struck him and he fell. He cried out: 'We are all lost if the train does not stop in five minutes.'

'The train will stop,' said Phileas Fogg, preparing to rush out of the carriage.

'Stay where you are, sir,' cried Passepartout. 'This is my job.'

Phileas Fogg had no time to stop the brave man who, opening one of the outer doors without being seen by the Indians, managed to climb down under one of the carriages.

While the fight went on, and with shots flying in the air over his head, Passepartout made his way forward under the carriages, holding on here and there, and crossing from one place to another until he got to the front part of the train. There, hanging on by one hand, he managed to undo the heavy iron hooks that joined the carriages to the engine. The train, now separated from the engine, began to run more and more slowly, while the engine flew forwards with still greater speed.

The train carried on for a few minutes but soon came to a stop less than 300 feet from the station. Hearing the shots, soldiers hurried up to the train. The Indians did not wait for them; they all ran off.

When the passengers were counted, it was found that three did not answer to their names, and among them was the Frenchman whose bravery had saved the train. What had happened to them? Had they been killed in the fight? Were they prisoners of the Indians? Nobody knew. One of the wounded passengers was Mr Proctor, who had fought bravely. He was taken with the others to the station, where they received every care.

Aouda was safe. Phileas Fogg was safe, too, although he had been fighting all the time. Fix was slightly wounded in the arm. But Passepartout was not to be found; and tears ran down the face of the young lady who owed her life to him now for the second time.

Mr Fogg stood there without speaking. He had to make a serious decision. If his servant had been taken prisoner, it was his duty to try to get him back.

'I shall find him, dead or alive,' he said simply to Aouda.

'Oh, Mr Fogg,' cried Aouda, taking his hands in hers and covering them with tears.

'I shall find him alive,' added Mr Fogg, 'if we waste no time.'

This decision meant that Phileas Fogg would lose everything. If he were only one day late he would fail to catch the boat at New York. His bet was lost. But it was his duty, and he had made up his mind.

A hundred soldiers and their captain were at the station in order to defend it against any attack by Indians.

'Sir,' said Mr Fogg to the captain, 'three people have disappeared.'

'Dead?' asked the captain.

'Dead or prisoners,' answered Phileas Fogg. 'That is what we must find out. Do you intend to follow the Indians?'

'That is a serious matter, sir,' answered the captain. 'These Indians may continue to run for two or three hundred miles. I cannot leave this station while it is under my protection.'

'Sir,' said Phileas Fogg, 'it is a question of the lives of three men.'

'Quite true, but can I put the lives of fifty men in danger to save three?'

'I don't know whether you can, but that is what you ought to do.'

'Sir,' answered the captain. 'I will not allow anybody here to teach me my duty.'

'Very well, then,' said Phileas Fogg coldly. 'I will go alone.'

'You!' cried Fix, who had come up to the two men. 'You intend to go after these Indians alone?'

'Do you think that I am going to leave that brave man who saved the lives of everybody here to die? I shall go.'

'Well, sir,' cried the captain. 'You will not go alone. No, you have a brave heart. Now! Who offers to join this gentleman? Thirty men are wanted!' he said, turning to his soldiers.

The whole company stepped forward. The captain only had to choose among them. Thirty were named, and an officer was put at their head.

'Thank you, Captain!' said Mr Fogg.

'You will allow me to come with you?' asked Fix.

'You may do as you like,' Fogg answered. 'But if you wish to be of real service to me, you will stay by the side of this lady and take care of her.'

The detective's face turned white. What! Separate himself from the man he was following so patiently? Let him go off alone into the wild country? Fix looked at Mr Fogg for a moment and then he looked away from Fogg's calm, serious face.

'I will stay,' he said.

A few minutes later Mr Fogg gave the young woman his bag, telling her to take great care of it; he shook hands with her, and went off with the officer and his little company of men.

Before leaving, he said to the soldiers, 'There's a thousand pounds for you if we save the prisoners.'

It was then a few minutes after midday.

Aouda had gone into the waiting room of the station, and there, alone, she thought of Phileas Fogg, this kind and brave man. He had given up his fortune and was now putting his life in danger. In her eyes he was a great and honourable man.

The detective Fix did not think that way at all, and could not hide his feelings. He walked up and down outside the station, feeling foolish for having let Fogg leave.

'I was a fool!' he thought. 'Fogg knows who I am! He has gone, and will not come back. Where shall I find him again? How could I have thought of letting him go; I, who have in my pocket the warrant for his arrest?'

Those were the thoughts of Fix while the hours slowly passed. He did not know what to do. Sometimes he felt like telling Aouda everything. Sometimes he felt like going off across the snow to catch this Mr Fogg. It would not be impossible to find him again. He could still follow the footprints of the soldiers, but before long the falling snow would cover them again.

Then Fix felt like giving everything up for lost and going straight back to England. If he decided to do that, there was nothing to prevent him, because at two o'clock, while the snow was falling heavily, the noise of an engine was heard coming from the east. But no train was expected from the east yet; the help for which they had asked could not come so quickly, and the train from Omaha to San Francisco would not arrive before the next day.

It was the engine of their train. It had rushed on for many miles, and then the fire had died for want of coal. There was no more steam, and an hour later the engine, running more and more slowly, had come to a stop twenty miles on the other side of Kearney Station.

The engine driver had not been killed; and after some time had passed, he had come to his senses. When he found that he was alone and that the engine was no longer pulling the train, he guessed what had happened. What he did not know was how the engine had become separated from the train.

He could go on to Omaha; that was the wisest thing to do. He could go back towards the train; that was dangerous, since the Indians might still be on the train. The driver soon made up his mind. He had to go back. Coal and wood were put on the fire; the water soon became hot again, and before long there was enough steam to make the engine run back to Kearney Station.

The passengers were pleased to see the engine once more at the head of the train. They could now continue their journey. Aouda, though, went up to the guard.

'You are leaving?' she asked.

'Immediately.'

'But the prisoners, our unfortunate travelling companions?'

'I am sorry we cannot wait for them. We are already three hours late.'

'And when does the next train come from San Francisco?'

'Tomorrow evening.'

'Tomorrow evening? But that will be too late. You must wait.'

'That is impossible,' answered the guard. 'If you want to come with us, you must get on the train now.'

'I shall not come,' answered the lady.

Fix had heard this talk. A few moments before, when there was no way of leaving, he had wanted to get away. Now that the train was there, and he had only to take his place in the carriage, he no longer wanted to leave. The struggle in his mind began all over again. He felt a terrible sense of failure.

The passengers had taken their places on the train. Among them was the wounded Mr Proctor, whose condition was serious. The noise of steam was heard. The bell rang, the train moved out of the station and was soon lost to view in the snow.

The detective had stayed behind.

Some hours passed. The weather was bad and it was very cold.

Fix was sitting on a seat in the station; he might have been asleep. Aouda, in spite of the snowstorm, kept going out of the room. She walked to the end of the platform, looked out and listened. But she saw and heard nothing.

Evening came. The little company of soldiers did not come back. Where were they? Had they been able to catch up with the Indians? Had there been a fight? The captain was very anxious, but tried not to show that he was worried.

Night came. The snow was no longer falling so heavily, but it got colder and colder. No sound could be heard.

All night Aouda, with a heavy heart and fearing the worst, walked about outside. In her imagination she could see a thousand dangers. Fix did not move, but he, too, was awake. At one point a man came up to him and said something. But Fix simply answered, 'No.'

In this way the night passed. The sun rose in a grey sky. Phileas Fogg and the soldiers had gone towards the south, but nothing was to be seen to the south except the snow.

The captain did not know what to do. Should he send a second company to help the first? At last he called one of his officers, and gave him orders to send out a few men towards the south – and at that moment shots were heard. Was it a signal? The soldiers rushed out and saw, half a mile away, the others coming back.

Mr Fogg was at the head of the company, and by his side were Passepartout and the two other travellers, saved from the Sioux.

There had been a battle ten miles to the south of Kearney. Shortly before the soldiers had reached them, Passepartout and his two companions had started fighting against those who had taken them prisoners. The Frenchman had already knocked three of them down when his master and the soldiers rushed up to help him.

At the station they were all welcomed with shouts of joy, and Phileas Fogg gave the soldiers the reward that he had promised them. Passepartout said more than once: 'I have certainly cost my master a lot of money!'

Fix looked at Mr Fogg without saying a word. It would be difficult to say what thoughts were passing through his mind. Aouda went up to Phileas Fogg, took his hands and pressed them between her own, unable to speak.

As soon as he reached the station, Passepartout looked round for the train. He was expecting to see it there ready to leave for Omaha, and hoped that they would be able to make up for the time that they had lost.

'Where's the train?' he cried.

'Gone,' answered Fix.

'And the next train?' asked Phileas Fogg.

'Will not come before this evening.'

'Ah!' was all that the gentleman answered.

Chapter 16   A Sledge with Sails

Phileas Fogg was now twenty hours late on his journey. Passepartout blamed himself for being the cause of the delay and refused to be comforted by anyone.

At that moment Fix walked up to Mr Fogg and said: 'Are you really in a hurry to get on?'

'I certainly am,' answered Phileas Fogg.

'You really want to get to New York by the 11th, before nine o'clock in the evening, when the boat leaves for Liverpool?'

'I do.'

'And if your journey had not been stopped by the attack on the train, you would have reached New York on the morning of the 11th?'

'I would. Twelve hours before the boat leaves.'

'Very well. You are twenty hours late. Between twelve and

twenty there is a difference of eight. Do you wish to make them up?'

'On foot?'

'No, on a sledge,' answered Fix. 'On a sledge with sails. A man has offered us the use of one.'

This was the man who had spoken to Fix during the night and whose offer Fix had refused.

Phileas Fogg did not answer, but Fix pointed to a man who was walking up and down in front of the station. Mr Fogg went up to him. A few moments later Phileas Fogg and this American, by the name of Mudge, entered a hut not far away. There Mr Fogg examined this strange sledge. It was built of wood, and was large enough to hold five or six people. It had a high mast, which carried a large sail. At the back was a sort of rudder by which the sledge could be made to go in any direction. It was a kind of ship, but instead of being made to sail through water, it sailed on ice or snow. During the winter, when trains are stopped by the snow, these sledges could travel between stations at great speed.

An arrangement was soon made with the owner of the sledge. A strong wind was blowing conveniently from the west. The snow was hard, and Mudge promised to take Mr Fogg to Omaha in a few hours. From Omaha there are many trains running on more than one railway line towards Chicago and New York. In this way it would be quite possible to make up for lost time, and there was no reason why the plan should not be tried.

As Aouda might suffer from the cold, Mr Fogg thought of leaving her with Passepartout at Kearney Station, and the Frenchman promised that he would bring her to Europe a little later by train and boat. But Aouda refused to be separated from Mr Fogg, and Passepartout was very happy with her decision. He had no wish to leave his master alone with Fix.

It would be difficult to say what Fix was thinking of all this. Had he changed his mind about Mr Fogg when he saw this gentleman come back, or did he still view him as an evil man who thought that after his journey round the world he would be safe in England? Perhaps he now had a higher opinion of Mr Fogg, but he was still determined to do his duty, and was as anxious as anybody to get back to England as soon as possible.

At eight o'clock the sledge was ready to start. The travellers took their places on it, well wrapped up and protected against the cold. The sail was raised and, with the wind behind it, the sledge flew forward at a speed of forty miles an hour.

The distance between Kearney and Omaha in a straight line was not more than 200 miles. If the wind did not drop, it would be possible to do this distance in five hours. If there were no accident, the travellers should be in Omaha by one o'clock.

It was a freezing journey. The travellers pressed against each other for warmth. The cold, made greater by the speed, prevented any possibility of speech. The sledge slid across the snow as lightly as a boat on the water. When the wind blew hard, it felt as if the sledge would be lifted up in the air. Mudge kept the sledge going in the right direction.

'If nothing breaks, we shall get there,' Mudge shouted to his passengers.

It was in Mudge's interest to get there in time, since Mr Fogg, as usual, had offered a big reward.

The country over which they passed was as flat as the sea. It looked like a very large frozen lake. There was nothing in the way and there were only two things to be afraid of: that the sledge might break or that the wind might drop. But the wind did not drop. It blew more strongly than ever. It made the mast bend, but the sledge was so solidly built that there was really no danger of anything breaking.

Passepartout now had a face as red as the setting sun. He began to hope again. Instead of getting to New York in the morning, they would get there in the evening, but they had a good chance of catching the boat. He was so happy that he was almost ready to shake hands with Fix and call him his friend. He did not forget that it was Fix himself who had suggested the sledge, which was the only way of getting to Omaha in time. But he still did not trust Fix; he felt that the detective was planning more of his old tricks.

One thing that Passepartout would never forget was the way in which Mr Fogg had gone back to save him from the Indians. To do that he had put his life and fortune in danger. No, he would never forget that.

At twelve o'clock Mudge saw that he had crossed the River Platte. He said nothing, but he was already sure that he would soon reach Omaha Station.

It took them exactly an hour. The sledge stopped, and Mudge pointed to a few hundred houses with snow-covered roofs.

'We are there,' he said.

Yes, they were really there. They had reached a station from which trains ran many times a day to the east.

Passepartout and Fix jumped off the sledge, glad to stretch their legs again after five hours without movement. They helped Mr Fogg and the young woman to climb down. Phileas Fogg gave the promised reward to Mudge, Passepartout shook his hand as if he were an old friend, and, wishing him well, they all hurried to the station.

A train was ready to leave, and Mr Fogg and his companions only just had time to jump into a carriage. They had seen nothing of Omaha, but Passepartout thought that was nothing to be sorry about.

The train passed at great speed through the countryside separating them from Chicago. The next day, the 10th, at four o'clock in the evening, they reached this famous city, which had already been rebuilt after the terrible fire that had destroyed it a few years earlier.

Nine hundred miles separate Chicago from New York, but

there were plenty of trains. Mr Fogg and his companions had only to get down from their train and to step into another. The engine started off at full speed as if it knew that Mr Fogg had no time to lose. The train flew through Indiana, Ohio, Pennsylvania and New Jersey.

At last the passengers saw the Hudson River, and on 11th December, at a quarter past eleven in the evening, the train came to a stop at the station on the river bank opposite the offices of the Steamship Company.

Chapter 17   Mr Fogg Tries to Find a Ship

The steamship *China* had left for Liverpool three-quarters of an hour earlier!

When it left New York, the *China* seemed to have taken with it Mr Fogg's last hope.

No other boat would suit his plan. The French boat would be leaving only on the 14th, two days later. The German boat was not going directly to Liverpool or London; it would be calling at a French port – and Mr Fogg would not be able to get from there to London in time.

One steamer, it is true, would be leaving the next day, but it was no use considering that one, because it was a slow boat, using sails rather than steam.

Passepartout was extremely upset. Three-quarters of an hour too late! It was his fault, he thought. Instead of helping his master, he had succeeded in making him late. When he looked back on all the things that had happened during the journey from London, when he added up all the money spent uselessly, when he thought of losing the bet, he felt completely to blame.

But Mr Fogg did not blame him and said simply: 'Well, we will think about the matter tomorrow.'

The travellers went to a hotel, but Mr Fogg was the only one who slept.

The next day was December 12th. From the 12th, at seven in the morning, to the 21st, at 8.45 in the evening, there were nine days, thirteen hours and forty-five minutes left. If, then, Phileas Fogg had set out the night before on the *China*, one of the fastest ships of the Steamship Company, he would have got to Liverpool, and then to London, in time.

Phileas Fogg left the hotel alone, having told his servant to wait for him and to let Aouda know that she must be ready to leave at any moment.

Mr Fogg went to the port and looked among the ships for any which were getting ready to sail. He found more than one; for in this busy port there is not a day when a hundred boats do not leave for every part of the world. But most of these were sailing boats, and they would not suit Phileas Fogg.

At last he noticed a fine-looking steamer. The clouds of smoke that she was sending out showed that she was making her final preparations.

Phileas Fogg called for a small boat, got into it, and in a few moments found himself at the side of the *Henrietta*. The captain was on board, and came immediately at Phileas Fogg's request. He was fifty years old, a rough-looking, unpleasant man. His large eyes, red hair and large body did not give him an attractive appearance.

'The captain?' asked Mr Fogg.

'I am he.'

'I am Phileas Fogg, of London.'

'And I am Andrew Speedy, of Cardiff.'

'You are about to leave?'

'In an hour.'

'You are heading for . . . ?'

'Bordeaux.'

'You have passengers?'

'No passengers. Never have passengers. I prefer goods. Goods don't get in the way, and they don't talk.'

'Yours is a fast ship?'

'Between eleven and twelve miles an hour. The *Henrietta* is well known for its speed.'

'Will you take me and three other persons to Liverpool?'

'To Liverpool? You might as well say China.'

'I said Liverpool.'

'No!'

'No?'

'No. I am setting out for Bordeaux, and I shall go to Bordeaux.'

'Whatever the price?'

'Whatever the price.'

The captain spoke in a voice that showed it was useless to reason with him.

'But the owners of the *Henrietta*–' argued Phileas Fogg.

'The owners of the *Henrietta* are myself,' replied the captain. 'The ship belongs to me.'

'I will hire it from you.'

'No.'

'I will buy it from you.'

'No.'

Phileas Fogg kept calm. But the position was serious. In New York it was not as simple as it had been in Hong Kong, nor was it as easy dealing with the captain of the *Henrietta* as it had been with the captain of the *Tankadere*. Until now the gentleman's money had always been able to get over every difficulty. This time money failed.

They could not cross the Atlantic by balloon; that would be too dangerous and, in fact, impossible, so a way must be found of crossing the Atlantic in a ship. Phileas Fogg suddenly seemed to have an idea; he said to the captain: 'Well, will you take me to Bordeaux?'

'No, not even if you were to pay me forty pounds.'

'I will pay you four hundred pounds.'

'For each person?'

'For each person.'

'And there are four of you?'

'Four.'

Captain Speedy did not know what to think. Sixteen hundred pounds to be earned without changing any plans; it was well worth the trouble of forgetting his dislike of passengers. Besides, passengers at four hundred pounds each are no longer passengers, but valuable goods.

'I am leaving at nine o'clock,' said Captain Speedy simply, 'and you and your people will be here?'

'By nine o'clock we will be on board,' replied Mr Fogg.

It was half past eight. Fogg left the *Henrietta*, took a carriage back to the hotel, and picked up Aouda, Passepartout, and even Mr Fix, to whom he kindly offered transport. All this was done by the gentleman with the calmness which never left him even when he was in the greatest trouble.

By the time the *Henrietta* was ready to sail, all four were on board. An hour later the steamer left the Hudson River. During the day she steamed along the shore of Long Island, and then she went out onto the open sea.

At twelve o'clock the next day, 13th December, a man began giving orders to the ship's officers, telling them in what direction the ship had to go. You might suppose that this man was Captain Speedy. Not at all. It was Phileas Fogg! Captain Speedy himself was locked up in his cabin and was roaring with anger – which was not surprising.

What had happened was very simple. Phileas Fogg wanted to go to Liverpool; the captain would not take him there. Then

Phileas Fogg had agreed to pay to go to Bordeaux, and during the thirty hours that he had been on board he had spent money so cleverly and wisely that the officers and men – who very much disliked their captain – belonged to him. And that is why Phileas Fogg, and not Captain Speedy, was master of the ship; why the captain was shut up in his cabin; and why, lastly, the *Henrietta* was making her way not towards Bordeaux but towards Liverpool. Seeing Mr Fogg sail the ship, it was very clear that he had once been a sailor. But how this adventure would end, nobody could tell.

Aouda felt very anxious about it, although she said nothing. Fix was so surprised that he too said nothing. Passepartout found the whole affair extremely exciting!

'Between eleven and twelve miles an hour,' Captain Speedy had said, and this seemed to be true.

If, then, the sea did not get too rough, if the wind did not blow from the east, and if there was no accident to the ship, the *Henrietta* would in the nine days, counting from 12th December to the 2lst, cross the 3,000 miles separating New York from Liverpool.

At first conditions were good. The wind was not too strong, and blew from the right direction. The sails were raised, and the *Henrietta* travelled as fast as any of the regular steamers.

◆

Passepartout was very, very happy, preferring not to think about what might happen later. The officers and men had never seen anyone so happy and excited. He made friends with the sailors, calling them by all sorts of friendly names, and giving them all kinds of good things to drink. He made others feel as happy as himself. He had forgotten the past, with its troubles and dangers. He thought only of the end of the journey, which was so near, and he sometimes became terribly impatient.

Fix did not understand anything at all. The taking of the *Henrietta*, the buying of her officers and men, and Fogg behaving like a regular sailor – this was too much for him. He did not know what to think. But, after all, a man who began by stealing fifty-five thousand pounds could finish by stealing a ship. Of course, he really believed that Fogg was not going to Liverpool at all, but to some part of the world where a robber might find a safe place to live. This plan now seemed most reasonable, and Fix began to be sorry about having any involvement in the affair.

As for Captain Speedy, he kept on roaring in his cabin, and Passepartout, whose duty it was to give him his food, did it only with the greatest care, in spite of his great strength.

Chapter 18   Mr Fogg Buys the *Henrietta*

On the 13th they passed close by the island of Newfoundland. This is a dangerous part of the Atlantic. Here, particularly during the winter, there is a lot of mist. There were signs that the weather was going to change. During the night it had grown colder, and at the same time the wind began to blow from the south-east.

This was a misfortune. Mr Fogg, in order not to be driven off course, had to take down the sails and to use more steam. But the ship went more slowly because of the state of the sea. Long waves broke against the ship and made her roll violently. The wind grew stronger and stronger until it was blowing a storm. For two days Passepartout was very frightened. But Phileas Fogg was a daring sailor, who knew how to win battles against the sea. The *Henrietta*, whenever she could rise with the waves, passed over them, but the water often poured across her from end to end.

The next day, 16th December, was the seventy-fifth day that had passed since leaving London. The *Henrietta* was not seriously late, half of the crossing was almost over, and the worst part of it was certainly behind them. In summer, success would have been certain. In winter, they had to trust to the weather. Passepartout said nothing, but in his heart he had hopes. 'If we cannot depend on the wind,' he thought, 'we can at least depend on steam.'

On this day, though, the chief engineer came up from below, met Mr Fogg, and had a very serious talk with him. Without knowing why, Passepartout felt worried. He would have given one of his ears to have heard, with the other, what was being said. But he did catch a few of his master's words: 'You are certain of what you say?'

'I am certain, sir,' answered the other. 'Do not forget that, since we left, all our boilers have been at the highest possible temperature, and although we had enough coal to travel in the usual way from New York to Bordeaux, we have not enough to go under full steam from New York to Liverpool.'

'I will think the matter over,' replied Mr Fogg.

Passepartout understood, and was terribly frightened. The coal was coming to an end.

'Ah! If my master can get over that difficulty,' he said to himself, 'he will certainly be a great man!'

He could not help telling the detective the state of things.

'Then,' answered Fix, 'you believe that we are going to Liverpool?'

'Of course.'

'Fool,' answered Fix, as he turned away.

And now what was Phileas Fogg going to do? It was difficult to guess. But it appeared that this calm gentleman had decided on a plan, for that evening he sent for the engineer and said to him: 'Keep your fires burning, and keep going in the same direction until there's no more coal left.'

At about twelve o'clock Phileas Fogg ordered Passepartout to go and bring Captain Speedy to him. Passepartout did not like having to do that, and he went down below, saying to himself: 'It is quite certain that I shall find him completely wild with anger!'

A few minutes later Captain Speedy came running up on deck shouting and roaring. He looked as if he were going to burst.

'Where are we?' were the first words he said in his terrible anger. 'Where are we?' he roared again.

'Seven hundred and seventy miles from Liverpool,' answered Mr Fogg, with great calmness.

'Thief!' cried Andrew Speedy.

'I have sent for you, sir—'

'Robber!'

'Sir,' continued Phileas Fogg, 'I have sent for you to ask you to sell me your ship.'

'No!'

'I am going to burn her.'

'To burn my ship!'

'At least the wooden parts, since we have no more coal.'

'Burn my ship!' cried Captain Speedy, who was so angry now that he could hardly speak. 'A ship that is worth ten thousand pounds!'

'Here are twelve thousand pounds,' said Phileas Fogg, holding the money out to him.

The result of this offer was to make Andrew Speedy forget his anger and all his reasons for complaint against Mr Fogg. His ship was twenty years old. It might in fact be worth selling the ship.

'And I can keep what is left of the ship after you have burnt the wooden parts?' he asked, in a strangely soft voice.

'Yes, everything made of metal will still be yours.'

'Then I agree.' And Andrew Speedy took the money and counted it.

During this conversation Passepartout's face had turned white. Twelve thousand pounds spent, and Fogg was still going to give back to the seller all the metal parts; that is, almost the whole value of the ship.

When Andrew Speedy had put the money in his pocket, Mr Fogg said to him: 'Sir, all this will not surprise you when I tell you that I shall lose twenty thousand pounds if I am not in London on 21st December at a quarter to nine in the evening. Now I was not able to catch the regular steamer from New York, and since you would not take me to Liverpool–'

'And I did well to say no,' cried Andrew Speedy, 'because by doing so I have gained at least eight thousand pounds.'

'Now this ship belongs to me?' asked Fogg.

'Certainly, from top to bottom; that is to say, all the wood, you understand.'

'Very well. Cut away the wood and put it on the fires.'

One can easily imagine how much of this wood was needed to get enough steam.

The next day, 19th December, the sailors continued to burn what could be burnt. By the following day, the 20th, almost all the woodwork above the waterline had been burned. But on this day the coast of Ireland came into sight.

At ten o'clock in the evening the ship was passing Queenstown. Phileas Fogg had only twenty-four hours to reach London! This was the time that the *Henrietta* needed to reach Liverpool, and there was little or no more steam.

'Sir,' said Captain Speedy, who had come to be interested in Mr Fogg's plan, 'I am really very sorry for you. Everything is against you. We are only off Queenstown.'

'Ah!' said Mr Fogg. 'Those are the lights of Queenstown?'

'Yes.'

'Can we go into the port?'

'Not for three hours. Only at high water.'

'Let us wait,' Phileas Fogg replied calmly, without letting it be seen on his face that he had one last plan to help him succeed!

Queenstown is where the steamers coming from America leave the mail. The letters are carried to Dublin by express trains.

103

From Dublin they are sent to Liverpool by very fast ships, arriving in Liverpool twelve hours before the fastest ships of the steamship companies.

Phileas Fogg meant to use these twelve hours. Instead of reaching Liverpool by the *Henrietta* on the evening of the next day, he would be there by twelve o'clock, and so he would have enough time to get to London before a quarter to nine in the evening.

Towards one o'clock in the morning the *Henrietta* came into Queenstown port at high water, and Phileas Fogg, having received a most friendly shake of the hand from Captain Speedy, gave him what was left of his ship, which was still worth half of what he had sold it for!

The passengers landed immediately. They jumped into the train at Queenstown at half past one in the morning, reached Dublin just as it was beginning to get light, and hurried on board one of those famous steamers which, instead of rising with the waves, always pass right through them.

At twenty minutes to twelve, on 21st December, Phileas Fogg landed in Liverpool. He was now only six hours from London. But at that moment Fix walked up to him, put his hand on his shoulder, and said: 'Your name, I believe, is Phileas Fogg.'

'Yes.'

'In the name of the Queen, I arrest you.'

Chapter 19 Mr Fogg Is in Prison

Phileas Fogg was in prison. They had taken him to the police station in Liverpool and he was going to spend the night there. The next day he would be taken to London.

At the moment of the arrest Passepartout tried to throw himself on the detective, but he was held back by the waiting policemen. Aouda, terrified at what she saw, understood nothing, so Passepartout explained the matter to her. Mr Fogg, this honest and brave gentleman to whom she owed her life, had been arrested as a thief. The lady cried out that such a charge was impossible, but she soon saw that she could do nothing to save the one who had saved her.

As for Fix, he had arrested Mr Fogg because it was his duty to arrest him, whether he was guilty or not. The law would decide the matter.

Then the terrible thought came to Passepartout that it was he who was the cause of this misfortune. After all, why had he hidden the matter from Mr Fogg? When Fix had informed him, Passepartout, of who he was and what he was going to do, why had he not told his master? If his master had known what he was accused of, he could certainly have proved to Fix that he was not guilty. In any case Mr Fogg would not have helped Fix to follow him or borne the cost of his travelling! As he thought of his foolishness in saying nothing, the poor man felt terribly guilty. Tears poured from his eyes. It was painful to watch.

In spite of the cold, Aouda and he had stayed outside the police station. Neither of them would leave the spot; they were so anxious to see Mr Fogg once again.

Mr Fogg had lost everything just as he was going to win. He had reached Liverpool at twenty minutes to twelve on 21st December. He had until a quarter to nine to get to the Reform Club – that is to say, nine hours and fifteen minutes – and the journey to London was one of six hours.

Anybody who could have seen Mr Fogg in the police station would have found him sitting quietly, on a wooden seat, without anger and perfectly calm. There he waited. What was he waiting for? Had he any hope of success?

Mr Fogg had put his watch carefully on a table in front of him, and he looked at it from time to time. Not a word escaped from him. In any case his position was a terrible one. There were only two possibilities:

As an honest man, Phileas Fogg had lost everything that he owned.

As a dishonest man, he had been caught.

Had he any idea of escaping from his prison? Perhaps so, for at a certain moment he walked round the room examining it. But the door was solidly locked, and the window could not be opened. He sat down again and waited.

One o'clock struck. Mr Fogg noticed that his watch was two minutes faster than the clock.

Two o'clock. If he could board a train now, it would not be too late to get to the Reform Club by twenty minutes to nine.

At twenty-eight minutes to three, a noise was heard outside, a noise of opening doors. He could hear voices. The door opened, and he saw Aouda, Passepartout and Fix, who ran towards him. Fix was out of breath, his hair was in disorder. He could hardly speak.

'Sir . . . sir . . . forgive me . . . a mistake . . . somebody who looked like you . . . The thief . . . arrested three days ago . . . You . . . are . . . free!'

Phileas Fogg was free. He went up to the detective. He looked him full in the face, and then, making the only sudden movement that he had ever made in his life, knocked the unfortunate detective down.

Fix, lying on the ground, said nothing. He had got the reward that he deserved. Mr Fogg, Aouda and Passepartout went out. They threw themselves into a carriage and in a few moments reached Liverpool Station.

Phileas Fogg asked whether there was a train leaving for London. It was twenty minutes to three. The train had left thirty-five minutes earlier. Phileas Fogg then ordered a special train.

There were several engines ready for such a journey, but

arrangements could not be made immediately, and the special train could not leave before three o'clock.

At three o'clock, Phileas Fogg, having said something to the engine driver about a certain reward for speed, was on his way to London in the company of the young lady and his brave servant.

It was necessary to cover the distance between Liverpool and London in five hours. This is quite possible when the line is clear from end to end. But several times the train was forced to stop, and when the train came into the station at London, every clock showed the time to be ten minutes to nine.

Phileas Fogg, having completed his journey round the world, was five minutes late.

He had lost.

◆

The next day the people who lived in Savile Row would have been very surprised if they had been told that Mr Fogg had come home. The doors and windows were all shut, and the house did not look as if anyone were there.

When he had left the station, Phileas Fogg had given orders to Passepartout to buy what was necessary for meals and he had then gone home. He had received this final blow with his usual calmness. All was lost, and the detective was to blame. Having successfully done what he had hoped to do, in spite of all difficulties and dangers, and with time to do good on the way, to fail at the moment of reaching the end of his journey, to fail because of something most unexpected and which was no fault of his own; that was terrible. Hardly anything was left of the large sum that he had taken away with him. All the money he now had in the world was the twenty thousand pounds lying in his bank, and this he owed to members of the Reform Club. Having spent so much on his journey, the winning of the bet would not have made him any richer – and it is probable that he had not wished to become any richer – but the losing of the bet left him without any money at all. He had made up his mind, though. He knew what he was going to do.

A room in the house in Savile Row was prepared for Aouda, who was extremely unhappy. From certain words that she had heard Mr Fogg say, she guessed that he was thinking of putting an end to his life. For this reason Passepartout watched his master closely.

The night passed. Mr Fogg had gone to bed, but had he slept? Aouda could not sleep at all. Passepartout had watched, like a loyal dog, at his master's door all night.

Next morning Mr Fogg called him and told him to make Aouda's breakfast. He asked to be excused from seeing her, as he needed to put his business in order. He would not come down, but in the evening he would like to speak to Aouda for a few moments.

Passepartout, having received these orders, had only to carry them out. He looked at his master and was unable to leave the room. His heart was heavy. He blamed himself more than ever for this sad ending to the adventure. If only he had warned his master about Fix's plans, Mr Fogg would certainly not have brought the detective with him to Liverpool, and then . . .

'Master! Mr Fogg!' he cried. 'Blame me. It is my fault that–'

'I blame nobody,' answered Phileas Fogg in the calmest of voices. 'Go.'

Passepartout went to Aouda and gave the message.

'My good friend, do not leave your master alone – not for a moment. You say that he wants to see me this evening?'

'Yes. I think that he wants to make arrangements for your protection in England.'

'Then we'll wait,' said she.

During the day it was as if nobody were living in the house. Phileas Fogg did not go to the club. Why should he go to the club? His old companions there were not expecting him. As he had not appeared at the club the evening before, at a quarter to nine, his bet was lost.

At half past seven in the evening Mr Fogg asked whether Aouda would receive him, and a few moments later they were alone in the room.

For five minutes he said nothing. Then, raising his eyes, he said: 'Will you forgive me for bringing you to England? When I had the idea of bringing you away from the country that had become so dangerous for you, I was rich and expected to offer you a part of my fortune. Your life would have been happy and free. Now I am poor.'

'I know that, Mr Fogg,' answered the young lady, 'and I will ask you this: will you forgive me for having followed you, and – who knows – for having been one of the causes of your failure?'

'You could not have stayed in India, and for your safety it was necessary for you to get away.'

'Then, Mr Fogg,' she went on, 'it was not enough for you to save me from a terrible death – you thought it your duty to take care of my future.'

'That is so, but I have been unfortunate. In any case my plan is to give you the little that I have left.'

'But you, Mr Fogg, what will you do?'

'I am in need of nothing for myself.'

'But do you know what you are going to do?'

'I shall do what it is right for me to do.'

'In any case, a man such as you cannot ever be in real want. Your friends—'

'I have no friends.'

'Then I am sorry for you, Mr Fogg, for it is sad to be without friends. It is said that misfortune can be borne when there are two to bear it.'

'So it is said.'

'Mr Fogg,' she then said, getting up and holding out her hand to him, 'will you have me as your friend? Will you have me as your wife?'

At these words Mr Fogg stood up. For a moment he shut his eyes. When he opened them again, he said simply: 'I love you. Yes, I love you and am yours!'

He called Passepartout, who came and saw his master and Aouda holding hands. The Frenchman understood, and his face filled with joy.

Mr Fogg asked him whether it was too late for him to call on the Reverend Samuel Wilson to make arrangements for a marriage.

Passepartout smiled. 'It is never too late,' he said. It was five minutes past eight. 'It will be for tomorrow, Monday,' he added.

'For tomorrow, Monday?' asked Mr Fogg, looking at Aouda.

'For tomorrow, Monday!' she answered.

Passepartout ran out of the house.

Chapter 20   A Mistake in the Day

On the Saturday evening the five gentlemen had met at the Reform Club at eight o'clock.

When the clock showed twenty-five minutes past eight, Andrew Stuart got up and said: 'Gentlemen, in twenty minutes' time Mr Fogg must be here or he will lose his bet.'

'At what time did the last train from Liverpool reach London?' asked Thomas Flanagan.

'At twenty-three minutes past seven. The next train gets to London at ten minutes past midnight.'

'Well, gentlemen,' said Andrew Stuart, 'if Phileas Fogg had come by the 7.23 he would already be here. We may safely say that we have won the bet.'

'We must wait,' said one of the others. 'You know that Mr Fogg is a man of very exact habits. He never gets anywhere too late or too early. If he came into this room at the last moment I would not be surprised.'

'As for me,' said Andrew Stuart, 'even if I saw him I wouldn't believe it. He has certainly lost. The *China*, the only steamer by which he could have come from America in time, reached Liverpool yesterday. Here is the list of people who were on it, and the name of Phileas Fogg is not among them. I imagine that he has hardly reached America. He will be at least twenty days late.'

'That is certain,' said another. 'Tomorrow we shall only have to go to the bank and collect the money.'

The clock showed twenty minutes to nine.

'Five minutes more,' said Andrew Stuart.

The five friends looked at each other. Their hearts were perhaps beating a little faster than usual; even among those who were used to betting, this bet was for a very large sum of money.

'I would not give up my four thousand pounds,' said Andrew Stuart, 'if I were offered three thousand nine hundred and ninety-nine pounds for it!'

At that moment the clock showed sixteen minutes to nine. Only one minute more and the bet would be won. They began to count the seconds.

At the fortieth second, nothing happened. At the fiftieth second, nothing happened.

At the fifty-fifth second, a noise like thunder was heard outside the room – a noise of shouting.

At the fifty-seventh second, the door of the room opened and, before the hand of the clock reached the sixtieth second, Phileas Fogg appeared followed by a large crowd of people who had forced their way into the building. He said, in his usual calm voice: 'Here I am, gentlemen.'

Yes! Phileas Fogg himself.

It will be remembered that at five minutes past eight – just over twenty-three hours after the travellers had arrived in London – Passepartout had been sent by his master to the Reverend Samuel Wilson to make arrangements for a certain marriage to take place the next day. He had left the house full of joy and happiness. The Reverend Samuel Wilson was not at home, so of course Passepartout waited. He waited at least twenty minutes.

It was twenty-five minutes to nine when he left the minister's house. But in what a state! His hair in disorder and without a hat, running and running as nobody had ever run before, knocking people over as he ran. In three minutes he was back at the house in Savile Row, and he fell breathlessly into Mr Fogg's room. He could not speak.

'What's the matter?' asked Mr Fogg.

'Master... marriage... impossible.'

'Impossible?'

'Impossible... for tomorrow.'

'Why?'

'Because tomorrow... is Sunday!'

'Monday,' answered Mr Fogg.

'No... today... Saturday.'

'Saturday? Impossible!'

'Yes, yes, yes!' cried Passepartout. 'You have made a mistake of one day. We reached London twenty-four hours early. But we have only ten minutes!'

Passepartout took his master and pulled him out of the room. Phileas Fogg, carried off without having time to think, left the house, jumped into a carriage, promised a hundred pounds to the driver, and having run over two dogs and knocked against five other carriages, reached the Reform Club.

The clock pointed to a quarter to nine when he came into the room where the members were waiting.

Phileas Fogg had completed his journey round the world in eighty days. Phileas Fogg had won the bet of twenty thousand pounds.

But how could such a careful man have made such a mistake? How was it that he had believed it to be Saturday evening, 21st December, when it was only Friday, 20th December, seventy-nine days since he had left?

The reason for the mistake is very simple.

Phileas Fogg had made his journey by going east. As he travelled towards the sun, the days got shorter by four minutes every time he crossed one of the 360 degrees by which the earth is measured. In other words, while he saw the sun pass over him eighty times, the members of the Reform Club saw it pass only seventy-nine times.

That is why on that day, which was Saturday and not Sunday, the members were waiting for him. If he had travelled towards the west, he would have lost a day on the way and would have reached London one day late.

Phileas Fogg had won the twenty thousand pounds. But as he had spent about nineteen thousand on the way, he had made little profit. And of the thousand pounds that was left, he gave half to Passepartout and the other half to the unfortunate Fix, whom he now forgave.

That same evening Mr Fogg, as calmly and coldly as usual, said to Aouda: 'Do you still want to marry me?'

'Mr Fogg,' she answered, 'it is I who ought to ask you that question. You were poor; now you are rich.'

'Excuse me,' he said, 'but my fortune belongs to you. If you had not suggested this marriage, my servant would not have gone to the Reverend Samuel Wilson; I would not have known about the mistake in the day, and . . .'

'Dear Mr Fogg,' said the lady.

'Dear Aouda,' answered Phileas Fogg.

◆

The marriage took place forty-eight hours later and Passepartout, in a state of joy, had the place of honour by the lady's side at the church.

And what had Phileas Fogg gained by this journey?

'Nothing,' you may say.

Very well, nothing! Except a beautiful and loving wife who – strange as it may seem – made him the happiest of men.

And was that not worth a journey round the world?

ACTIVITIES

Chapters 1–4

Before you read

1 Imagine that you had to travel round the world in eighty days with another student, and you could only go by land and sea. Look at a map of the world and discuss these questions.

    a Starting from your nearest big city, which route would you take?

    b What type of transport would you use?

    c Which part of the journey would be the most difficult? Why?

2 Find these cities on a map of the world. (Some of them now have different names, so you may need to check on the Internet.)

    London Calais Brindisi Suez Aden Bombay Calcutta Hong Kong Yokohama San Francisco New York

3 Look at the Word List at the back of the book. Find words for:

    a people

    b types of transport

    c parts of a boat or ship

While you read

4 Put these events in Phileas Fogg's life in the right order. Number them 1–10.

    a He buys an elephant.   .....

    b He arrives in Suez.   .....

    c He sees an Indian princess.   .....

    d He arrives at Aden.   .....

    e He hears about a bank robbery.   .....

    f He arrives at the Pillaji temple.   .....

    g He meets an army officer.   .....

    h He employs a new servant.   .....

    i He makes a bet.   .....

    j He arrives in Bombay.   .....

5 Answer these questions.

Why does Phileas:
a go to the Reform Club every day?
b employ a new servant?
c want to travel around the world in eighty days?
d have his passport signed in different places?
e buy an elephant and hire a guide?
f go to the Pillaji temple?

Why does Passepartout:
g get into trouble in Bombay?
h say that Phileas has a kind heart?

Why does Mr Fix:
i follow Phileas?
j not arrest Phileas in Bombay?

6 Which of these words describe Phileas? Why?
punctual popular patient polite pessimistic peculiar
practical

7 Work with another student. Have this conversation at the Pillaji temple.

Student A: You are a priest at the Pillaji temple. Explain your customs to Phileas. Tell him why Princess Aouda must die.

Student B: You are Phileas. Show respect for the priest's customs, but try to persuade him to let the princess live.

Chapters 5–8

Before you read

8 Will Phileas and his companions save Princess Aouda? How?

While you read

9 Are these sentences true (T) or false (F)?

a Passepartout's plan saves Princess Aouda. .....

b Phileas and his companions travel to Allahabad by train. .....

c The guide thinks that Phileas is mean. .....

d Mr Fix has Phileas and Passepartout arrested in Calcutta. .....

e Phileas knows that his two thousand pounds will not be returned. .....

f Passepartout knows that Fix is a detective. .....

g The *Rangoon* arrives late in Hong Kong. .....

h Phileas takes Aouda to her uncle. .....

i Fix thinks that Passepartout is telling him the truth. .....

j Passepartout refuses to help Fix. .....

After you read

10 What misunderstandings are there between these people?

a Phileas and the judge in Calcutta

b Fix and Phileas

c Passepartout and Fix

11 How does Fix feel and why:

a when he first arrives in Calcutta?

b when the judge sends Phileas to prison?

c when Phileas offers bail?

d when Phileas gets on the *Rangoon*?

e when he hears about Aouda's uncle in Hong Kong?

f after his second conversation with Passepartout on the *Rangoon*?

g when bad weather hits the *Rangoon*?

h when he hears Phileas's conversation with the pilot in Hong Kong?

i when he arrives in Hong Kong?

j when Passepartout gets drunk?

12 Discuss these questions. What do you think?

    a Is Fix a good detective? Why (not)?

    b Should Passepartout tell Phileas about his conversations with Fix? Why (not)?

    c If you were Aouda, would you want to go with Phileas to Europe? Why (not)?

Chapters 9–12

Before you read

13 What problems do you think Passepartout's drunkenness will cause Phileas?

While you read

14 Circle the correct word.

    a Phileas is *annoyed / calm* when he realises that the *Carnatic* has left without him.

    b Phileas finds a boat to take him to *Shanghai / Yokohama*.

    c *Seven / Eight* people sail on the *Tankadere*.

    d Without the storm, the *Tankadere* would have travelled *thirty / seventy* more miles.

    e Passepartout travels to Yokohama on the *Carnatic / Tankadere*.

    f In Yokohama, Passepartout plans to work as a *cook / singer*.

    g Phileas *knows / does not know* where to find Passepartout.

    h Passepartout *tells / does not tell* Phileas about Fix.

    i The second part of the journey will probably be *easier / more difficult* than the first.

    j Fix cannot arrest Phileas on the steamer for San Francisco because he *is outside British law / does not have a warrant*.

After you read

15 How are these important in this part of the story?

    a John Bunsby   **c** acrobats

    b a cannon   **d** British soil

16 Who is talking to whom? What are they talking about?

    a 'I have not the honour of knowing you.'

    b 'You will not be afraid?'

    c 'It really starts its journey at Shanghai.'

    d 'I count it as part of the cost of the journey.'

    e 'Signal to them.'

    f 'Why are you dressed like that?'

    g 'You see that my plan has changed.'

    h 'We can help each other.'

17 Match the two parts of the sentences.

    a Phileas does not feel worried although
Passepartout …   .....

    b Phileas does not look disappointed although
the *Carnatic* …   .....

    c Fix says that he feels disappointed although he …   .....

    d Phileas cannot find another boat although he …   .....

    e John Bunsby refuses to sail to Yokohama although
Phileas …   .....

    f Phileas can still catch the American steamer
although he …   .....

    g Phileas offers to pay for Fix's journey although he …   .....

    h The *Tankadere* reaches Shanghai although it …   .....

    i Passepartout jumps down from the stage although
he …   .....

    j Fix behaves calmly although Passepartout …   .....

    1) makes him a good offer.

    2) has hit him several times.

    3) has already left.

    4) hardly knows him.

    5) searches for hours.

    6) has been a stormy journey.

    7) is in the middle of a human pyramid.

    8) cannot get to Yokohama.

    9) secretly feels happy.

    10) has not returned.

18 Work with another student. Have this conversation about Phileas.

    Student A: You are Passepartout. You see that Aouda has fallen in love with Phileas. You think that life as his wife might be difficult. Tell her why.

    Student B: You think that Phileas would be a perfect husband. Tell Passepartout why.

Chapters 13–16

Before you read

19 What problems do you think Phileas might meet travelling by train across the United States in winter?

While you read

20 Write in the missing word.

    a In San Francisco, Passepartout buys some ....

    b The streets are crowded because there is an ....

    c The journey from San Francisco to New York should take .... days.

    d The train stops for three hours because .... are crossing the line.

    e There is another delay because of an unsafe ....

    f Phileas's fight with Stamp W. Proctor is interrupted by the sound of .... from outside the train.

    g .... saves all the passengers' lives.

    h Phileas looks for .... with thirty soldiers.

    i Fix decides to wait for Phileas with ....

    j Phileas and his companions travel to .... by sledge.

After you read

21 There are twelve mistakes, which are <u>underlined</u>, in this short
description of this part of the story. Correct them.

In San Francisco, <u>Phileas Fogg</u> is hit by a big man with <u>dark</u> hair.
Later, after buying new clothes, Phileas and his companions get on
the train for <u>Chicago</u>. Fix suggests <u>singing songs</u> to stop Phileas
seeing Stamp W. Proctor, his <u>friend</u>. However, after <u>a fifteen-mile
walk in the snow to avoid</u> an unsafe bridge, Phileas sees Proctor
and agrees to have a <u>drink</u> with him. They are interrupted when
the train is attacked by <u>robbers</u>. Passepartout is taken prisoner
but Phileas rescues him while Aouda waits <u>alone</u> for them at Fort
Kearney Station. Finally they travel to <u>Chicago</u> by <u>balloon</u> because
<u>they do not trust the train driver</u>.

22 How are these places or people important in this part of the
story?

- **a** Oakland Station
- **b** Aouda
- **c** Medicine Bow
- **d** Foster
- **e** Plum Creek
- **f** Fort Kearney Station
- **g** Mudge
- **h** Omaha
- **i** Chicago

23 Discuss these questions.

- **a** What does Fix really think of Phileas? Why?
- **b** What does Passepartout think of the United States? Why?
- **c** Does Phileas show any bad qualities in this part of the story?
  What are they?

Chapters 17–20

Before you read

24 Discuss these questions with another student.

- **a** Do you think that Phileas will win his bet with the gentlemen at
  the Reform Club?
- **b** What problems might he have on the last part of his journey?
- **c** What do you think will happen to Aouda when she arrives in
  England?

25 Who or what are these sentences about?

    a Phileas cannot find one. ....

    b He feels guilty. ....

    c He is locked in his cabin. ....

    d Phileas buys it. ....

    e Phileas uses it as fuel. ....

    f Phileas and his companions arrive there at dawn. ....

    g Phileas hits him. ....

    h Aouda and Passepartout are worried that Phileas might do this. ....

    i Passepartout cannot find him. ....

    j If Aouda had not suggested this, Phileas would have lost his bet. ....

After you read

26 At the end of the story, which of these people are happy? Why (not)?

    a Phileas

    b Passepartout

    c the captain of the *Henrietta*

    d the gentlemen at the Reform Club

    e Aouda

    f Fix

27 How do these help Phileas to win his bet?

    a Andrew Speedy

    b the crew of the *Henrietta*

    c an express train

    d a steamer carrying mail

    e a special train

    f Aouda

    g Passepartout

    h his journey eastwards

28 Work with another student. Have this conversation at the Reform Club at the end of the story.

    Student A: You are a gentleman at the Reform Club. You think that Phileas's journey around the world was a waste of time and money. Tell him why.

    Student B: You are Phileas. You think that your journey was a great success. Tell the gentleman why.

Writing

29 Describe Phileas's and Passepartout's seven-day journey from London to Suez.

30 You are Fix (Chapter 7). Write a report on Phileas Fogg's activities in India. Explain why you think that he is the London bank robber, and why you are going to follow him to Hong Kong.

31 You are John Bunsby (Chapter 10). Describe your four-day journey to Shanghai in your diary. Write a paragraph for each day.

32 You are Passepartout (Chapter 15). Write a letter to a friend, giving your opinions on life in the United States. Would you like to live there? Why (not).

33 Passepartout thinks that he is to blame for Phileas losing his bet (Chapter 20). Do you agree with him? Why (not)?

34 You are a journalist. Write about Phileas Fogg's return to London and his wedding for your newspaper.

35 'Phileas Fogg is a perfect English gentleman but a sad human being.' Do you agree with this statement? Why (not)? Use examples from the story to support your opinion.

36 You are Phileas. Passepartout wants to return to France, and has asked you for a letter of recommendation. Write your letter, describing for his future employer Passepartout's qualities as a servant.

37 You are Phileas. You need another servant after Passepartout leaves. Write your advertisement. What qualities are you looking for? What are the conditions of employment and rewards of the job?

38 Did you enjoy this story? Would you recommend it to other readers? Why (not)? Write about it for your school/college magazine.

Answers for the Activities in this book are available from the Pearson English Readers website. A free Activity Worksheet is also available from the website. Activity worksheets are part of the Pearson English Readers Teacher Support Programme, which also includes Progress tests and Graded Reader Guidelines. For more information, please visit: www.pearsonenglishreaders.com

WORD LIST

acrobat (n) someone who entertains people by doing difficult physical actions like jumps and balancing acts

arrest (n/v) the act of taking someone to a police station because they are believed to be guilty of a crime

bail (n) money paid so that someone can leave prison until their trial

balloon (n) a large, strong bag filled with hot air or gas that can carry passengers below it

bay (n) a part of a coastline where the land curves in

boiler (n) a large container for boiling water to provide steam for an engine

buffalo (n) an animal like a cow, that lives in Asia and Africa

cabin (n) a small room on a ship where you sleep

canal (n) a long, narrow man-made waterway for ships and boats

cannon (n) a large gun, fixed to the ground or on wheels

carriage (n) a vehicle pulled by horses; one of the parts of a train where passengers sit

companion (n) someone who you spend a lot of time with

consul (n) an official who lives in a foreign city and helps citizens of his or her own country who are there

deck (n) the flat top part of a ship that you can walk on

honourable (adj) behaving in a way that is morally right, which makes people respect you; **the Honourable** is a title for the children of some upper-class men and for some government officials

mast (n) a tall pole on which the sails of a boat are hung

pyramid (n) a very old stone building with four walls that go up towards a point at the top

reverend (n) a minister in the Christian church

revolver (n) a type of small gun

roar (v) to make a deep, loud, continuous noise

rudder (n) a flat part at the back of a boat that is turned to change the direction of the boat

silk (n) soft, fine cloth made from a substance produced by a kind of small animal

sledge (n) a vehicle used for travelling on snow

soil (n) the top layer of the earth, in which plants grow

steamer (n) a ship that uses steam power

telegram (n) a message sent using electrical signals

temple (n) a building where people go to pray in some religions

tightrope (n) a rope or wire high above the ground that a performer walks on

trade (n) the kind of work that someone does; a **trader** buys and sells quantities of goods

warrant (n) an official document that allows the police to take someone to the police station and keep them there